TO CATCH AN ANGEL

Adventures in the world

ROBERT RUSSELL

To Catch an Angel

I cannot see

THE VANGUARD PRESS, INC. *New York*

This book is dedicated to my brothers and sisters,
Larry, Bud, Jack, Jimmy, Mary, and Hunnie,
and to the warm memory of our father and mother

Contents

Three: THE MIDDLE SLOPE

Preface

Ever since I was a young child, people have stared at me. Knots of window-shoppers are suddenly silent as I pass, and when they think me out of earshot they say, "Isn't it a shame!"

And when someone helps me across a crowded intersection, his curiosity cannot be restrained.

"What's it like? Just darkness, eh? Always dark like midnight, I suppose? It must be very strange. But, then, you have a sixth sense, don't you? All you people do. Very strange!"

"Well," I asked myself, "am I so strange?"

I have come to the conclusion that they are right—I am peculiar. I am convinced, also, that those window-shoppers, if they considered the question seriously, would come to the same conclusion about themselves. For we are all oddities, all peculiar, all individuals. But the loneliness of being separate and distinct is softened by our sharing of a common life. We all thrill to the same hopes and cower before the same monsters, and, most of all, we are all forced to act on insufficient knowledge. We are forced irrevocably to commit ourselves financially, emotionally, intellectually, and spiritually without being able to foresee the consequences. As parents, as teachers, as statesmen, we are all the blind leading the blind.

Perhaps this is why people are especially interested in a blind person—because in his uncertain gait they unconsciously recognize a symbol of their own uncertain progress toward the unseeable. Therefore, my story is your story also. True, there are differences in the circumstances and events, but behind those superficial differences lies the common theme of our lives—the leaving of the familiar, in which we rest secure, for the sake of an uncertain future.

Man is an animal that walks spiritually as well as physically, and to walk is to push the world behind one. We are all blind men in our wild and rugged country in which, with each step, we hazard all we are. This book is the story of the first part of my life; so it is the story of movement, for while we are young nature is so strong in us that it forces us to accept the challenge of the unknown.

One: THE VALLEY OF
THE SHADOW

1. The Descent

In the 1870's Binghamton was a raw and boisterous town. Twenty years earlier it had been only a quiet settlement perched on the tongue of land that juts out where the Chenango and Susquehannah Rivers meet in south-central New York State just north of the Pennsylvania line. It had been a trading center drawing its life from the river traffic and acting as a market place for the farms that dotted the rich valleys. In the seventies, though, the railroads had pretty well put an end to such traffic, and only an occasional barge crept slowly along, drawn by a mule or two.

With the coming of the railroad, the town sprang to life as though waking from a river dream. There was hurry and bustle everywhere as the little place grew. It leaped across both rivers and shot long rows of frame houses along the banks like arms stretching out to welcome the new business and the coming prosperity.

On one of the side streets near the river, my father, Jim Russell, was born, the second son of a happy-go-lucky immigrant shoemaker and his hard-working Irish wife. Jim had inherited his mother's industry and practicality, and from his father a sense of humor and the capacity to dream. In him these dissonant qualities were tempered and united.

Jim left school when he was fourteen and started to work to help keep the family solvent. He found his way into a large cigar company and went into its bookkeeping department, where, in a few years, he had worked his way to being head bookkeeper. For a young man in his early twenties he was doing well, and he would obviously move up.

One night at a dance he met May Clark. She had come up from Washington, D.C., to visit some of her cousins near Binghamton. Her hair was a soft waterfall of reddish gold, and her eyes sparkled and danced with a spirit as flexible as it was strong. She was only fifteen, and although he was twenty-five, he went home from the dance with his mind made up. He would marry May Clark, but he would not be another man's bookkeeper when he asked for her hand. He would be independent before he spoke. Refusing all the offers his employers made in the hope of keeping him, he left his job. In 1902 he and a friend, Dan O'Brien, became partners, and the jewelry store of

Russell and O'Brien was, for forty-five years, one of the finest small shops on Court Street.

Five years later he and May Clark were married. In the years that followed, she bore him four sons in quick succession—Larry, Bud, Jack, and Jimmy. Then came two girls, Mary and Hunnie. I was born in 1924, the last of their seven children.

My earliest recollections are of our large home at Number 13 Edward Street. It was an enormous three-story house, green with cream trim. It was not magnificent, but it was substantial—ample proof of the good sense and simple tastes of the wealthy lumber merchant who had built it for his own family. There was a spacious front porch, a big back yard, and a genuine barn with stalls for the horses and plenty of carriage room. This was to be the home of our 1928 Packard.

One day I was playing hide-and-seek with Hunnie. I was crouched beside the big red brick chimney that jutted out from the side of the house, leaving a small corner in which to hide. Suddenly I heard the quiet purr of a powerful motor, and a vast black car glided down our driveway. My father was behind the wheel, and he was smoking his pipe. He looked like a small boy who shouts, "Look what I've got!"

"Where's your mother, Rob?" he asked, but before I could collect myself to reply she came out of the house in her apron, amazement and delight on her face. The car was really ours. We must go for a ride, and I had to get cleaned up for the occasion. My mother washed and scrubbed me in a way that only the mother of seven can wash and scrub a small boy. She produced a new suit of brilliant green that she had been keeping for Sunday, and off we went, cruising around the town as though we owned it. I was in heaven.

The long rows of white houses with their neat front lawns lay dozing in the afternoon sun. The stray bands of children playing on the sidewalks stopped their games when they caught sight of beautiful us in our beautiful car. Housewives relaxing on their front porches stood up as we approached and walked to the railings to get a better look at our black magnificence.

When we got home, the whole family collected to congratulate one another. They were so busy and pleased with themselves that they did not notice me crawl off the porch and slip round the side of the house. Once out of their sight, I made a dash for the barn and the car. Its splendor overwhelmed me. I ran my hands over the glossy black hood and fenders. Had there ever been anything more wonderful?

I sat down on the floor beside one of the wheels. They, too, were black, but not completely. There were two concentric circles of brilliant green around the silver hub cap. The combination of the black, the green, and the silver stirred my creative faculty. How beautiful are thy wheels with green and silver and black! But oh!—even more beautiful thy wheels with green and silver and black and . . . blue!

The very thing. I leaped to my feet, ran over to a corner of the barn where I thought I remembered . . . yes, there it was . . . the old can of blue enamel, and open, too. I took a small stick used for stirring paint and made it do for a brush. The paint was so thick that huge gobs clung to my tool, and I set feverishly to work improving the design and pattern on the wheel.

I must have worked very rapidly, for I soon finished the wheel and had time and energy left to begin on the front fenders and the hood; but, like so many masters of old, I was given neither the time nor the opportunity to complete my handiwork. Footsteps came down the driveway, the barn door slid back, there was a stifled cry, and a firm hand gripped my collar. And then! Oh, alas for my art and alas for my bottom! Both suffered sorely on that evil day. My new suit, too; my lovely new green and now blue suit. My mother pulled it off, rolled it into a tight bundle, and shoved it into the garbage can.

Despite all the turpentine and elbow grease of four stalwart brothers, at the end of ten years of hard service the car still bore the traces of my hour of glory.

My confinement resulting from that misdeed was short-lived, and I was soon playing with the other children on the block. One boy named Charlie and I were great friends, and soon after the painting of the Packard he and I noticed that a family was moving out of a house just up the street from Number 13.

We couldn't wait for them to leave. When the last truckload of furniture was gone we set out on a tour of exploration to see what the movers had overlooked.

We slipped into the house and began our search. As we crept about on our hands and knees to escape detection through the curtainless windows, my heart beat fast with excitement and fear. The daring of our expedition filled me with dread. The brilliant sunshine on the bare and polished floors made pools of liquid gold whose edges melted into the deepening shadows in the corners; the dark closet stood with its door ajar; and the stairway in the hall led up into the gloom and silence of the second floor.

It was not because we imagined the house to be haunted that we were frightened; it was because we knew it to be empty. We had a whole vacant house to people with the creatures of our imagining.

I could not refine and select the details of my creations. I had no clear sense of the kind of phantoms that filled the house. They were all about me—tall, dark shapes in the shadowy corners; winged apparitions flitting through the silence of the second floor; tiny genii whirling in the shafts of sunlight. I was appalled and entranced by the sudden and huge activity of this strange power within me, this fantastic imagination.

Our whispers and silent agreement not to venture upstairs proved that Charlie was frightened too, though neither of us spoke of it.

So we scoured the downstairs and to our dismay found absolutely nothing. We crept through the back door to continue our search in the garage. Before we reached it, however, Charlie gave a cry of pleasure. His keen eye had detected a box under the back porch. We hauled it out, and to our delight it contained an old croquet set. We forgot our plans to explore any further and rushed home with our prize. Because Charlie was bigger and older than I and because he had seen it first, I was convinced that the set rightfully belonged to him and not to me.

He handed me one of the mallets before taking his

treasure home. I was quite content and dashed off with it, set upon performing great deeds. But what could I do? What did people do with mallets, anyway? A mallet isn't much use without croquet balls, and Charlie had those. But it looks very like a hammer, so I would use it like a hammer. There was nothing around the back of our house that I thought would respond to hammering, nothing except the windows on the back porch, and—well, I had had quite enough trouble lately so I sat down on the bottom step of the porch to hammer stones.

I sat on the step, mallet in hand, a small boy completely absorbed in his game—carefully selecting the stones and placing them in just the right way on the gray concrete walk skirting the dark green lawn, and then, taking deliberate aim, bringing down my mallet with all my might. Carpenters were wonderful men, and one day, maybe, I would grow up to hammer nails with the best of them, *just—like*—THAT! And then it happened.

The handle of the mallet split, and a flying splinter pierced the pupil of my left eye. Scrambling to my feet, I ran screaming up the stairs to the back door, the blood streaming down my face. Jimmy rushed out. He shouted for my mother, and in a moment I was bandaged and sitting beside her in a taxi on the way to the doctor's. He must have given me a sedative, for I remember nothing more.

At that time doctors did not know exactly how infection, which developed in my left eye, was communicated from the injured eye to the other. The only measure that could be taken to prevent a sympathetic reaction was to remove the left eye. This seemed a drastic step to the doctor and to my parents when, after all, it might be altogether unnecessary.

During the weeks that followed my father asked me the same question each evening at the dinner table.

"What color is my tie tonight, Rob?"

Gradually the table between us grew wider and wider, the bright colors softened and faded until they melted into a blur. Hoping against hope that only the intensity of the light was at fault, my father would get up from his chair and walk around the end of the table so I could get a better look. The light slowly grew worse, and finally he was leaning over me where I sat.

"Now, have a good look, Rob. You can see it now, can't you?"

I strained desperately to see what he wanted me to see because I knew it was somehow very important to him. But, try as I might, the light was just too poor.

So one lovely summer evening I was taken for a ride in the Packard by my brother Jack to play miniature golf. After a brief visit to the course we stopped at the hospital and I realized then something terrible was going to happen.

I was operated on that same night. My left eye was removed.

I awoke the next day in a vast white bed that seemed higher from the floor than I was tall. When my nurse had left the room, I crawled to the edge of the bed and fell onto the cold floor. I tried desperately to get to my feet, for I was determined to leave the wretched place and go home. But my legs would not carry me even so far as the door, and I wept with shame. In terror, I tried to get back into the bed but it was too high.

It would be wrong to say my nurse caught me, for being caught implies I could have escaped if I had only been quicker. She picked me up and put me back between the cold sheets with many warnings about what she would do if I tried it again. She need not have worried. I would lie still.

For the first time in my life I had wanted to do something with all my being. I had commanded my flesh, and it had failed me. I was ashamed of my weakness, but, even more, I was indignant at the refusal of my body to do what I had insisted. I realized then that my body could not perform the imperative commands of my spirit. This experience was the door through which I passed out of my childhood.

To be human is to be limited, and, though our limitations are different, the process of learning to live with them is the same. As a child struggling to escape from, and then return to, the vast, cold hospital bed, I was facing limitation and I would have to learn to live with it.

At home, I spent several months in bed. My right eye throbbed and burned constantly. My mind was numb. I was submerged in a dark sea to whose surface I rose only for glimpses of my mother sitting on the chair beside my bed and to hear my father's footsteps outside my door, where he spent every night.

Gradually the pain diminished and I began to regain my strength. One day a woman came to visit my mother and me. I grew more and more restless, because they both talked and talked and would not let me go back to my play. Finally the woman produced a large book, laid it open on the piano bench, and asked me to read to her.

The enormous letters were only blue blurs on the gray page. After a few more minutes of conversation, the woman took her book and disappeared.

"How would you like to go to school, Rob?" my mother asked. The idea of meeting new children filled me with dread, and I was wretched when told I should not come home even for lunch.

"Wouldn't it be fun to take your lunch to school and eat with lots of other boys and girls?" I saw through the question and cried. I was to be entered in a sight-saving class where all the children had defective vision, and where all the equipment was specially made so as not to strain weak eyes. I never did go to that school—not because I had protested against it, but because it soon became all too clear that the little sight I still had in my right eye was fading fast. In short, I would soon have no sight to save.

Scenes from this period stand out like snapshots:

I am in the back yard looking up at the sky. Every nerve is taut with the looking. White clouds, freshly laundered, are strewn carelessly on a background of the deepest blue. They are not still. They move like a fleet of Spanish galleons under full canvas, sailing with slow majesty across the softest of oceans on a light spring breeze.

It is a summer afternoon, green and gold. Edward Street has been freshly tarred and graveled. It is a shining black river flowing under a canopy of leaves. I am sitting on the curb staring down at the black diamonds that glisten and sparkle. Over by the other curb the milkman's horse has left a dark brown heap at which a cluster of neighborhood sparrows have convened. A big blue car rolls around the corner of North Street toward them. A brown fountain jets up and plumes out, and the sparrows flutter back into the whispering green. As the car swings around the next corner, my street is empty again, except for the green, the gold, the glistening black, and the peace and the heat of a summer afternoon.

It is winter. Snow has been falling fast during the night and is still coming down when I get up and run to the warm kitchen where my mother is cooking breakfast amid smells of bacon and coffee.

"Look at the snow, Rob," she says. And I go to the window and press my nose against the cold glass: a clean world, absolutely pure, is covered with white silence, and the snow is still coming down. I try to see into the middle—not through, but into the middle of the snow-storm. I see the mystery. The center is the mystery of pure, white silence, the tumultuous privacy of the storm.

I am grateful for these snapshots, because I saw with the eyes of a child. The world never became so familiar to me that I learned to ignore it.

They say that no one noticed sunsets until Turner saw them and painted them, and that now all of us see sunsets through his eyes. I believe it. Emerson says that if the stars appeared only once in a thousand years, they would be the marvels of the universe. But they appear every night. For me, the sky, the snow, and the stars appeared once only so I saw them plain. In my fifth year I looked with failing eyes upon the world I was about to leave.

At six, while the shadowy borders crept closer and closer, finally to engulf me, I slipped quietly into that land where there is no light, where the yellow sunshine no longer lies in pools of liquid gold on polished mahogany, where white lilacs no longer hang like ghostly lamps in a green night. Here the sunshine is warmth, the mahogany smoothness, and the lilac a deep well of fragrance into which one can plunge and drowse away one's life.

But this change of the sun from light to warmth, of the mahogany from color to smoothness, and of the lilac tree next door from whiteness to fragrance, was not dramatic. It was slow, very slow; it took more than a year.

I was too young to be firmly committed to living in a world of light; and so, as I wandered through the land of evening and at last crossed its borders, my ears became accustomed to the darkness; and as my dependence upon them grew, so did their power. So gradually did they accept the function of my eyes that there was no specific time when I knew the change had been completed. There was no crisis. I did not know when I became a citizen of the night.

2. Black Crow, White Crow

But not all crises are physical. No one lives alone, and the citizens of the day were deciding where I should pass my life.

Black crows herd the white crows together, put them in a special place, and insist they stay there. Then the blacks have the comfort of adopting a general policy toward the whites; but because there are no white crows left among them, the policy is based on ignorance. As the whites gradually develop a culture of their own, their tiny world begins to seem like the real one; they feel ill at ease when chance throws them into company with a member of the other flock.

I was separated out from the blacks in a neighbor's back yard.

Up the block from 13 Edward Street lived a little girl. She had a lovely apple tree out in back. It had sweet fruit and low branches into which even the youngest of us could scramble.

One afternoon seven or eight of us were playing there. I was alone beneath the tree while the others wandered about in search of amusement. For me they were only blurred shapes, seen through murky glass. Two of the shapes drew together. I heard them whispering; then one of them bent down and straightened up. Suddenly an apple whizzed past my head and rolled away on the grass. Another child picked it up and hurled it back. *Thud!* And an apple bounced off my shoulder.

"Hey," I called, "cut it out, will you?"

There was a soft ripple of children's laughter. A shape darted forward to where the apple had fallen, stopped, and darted back. *Whack!* came the apple against my cheek, and tiny bright fountains of delight danced in the afternoon sunshine.

Bang! another apple struck the back of my head. My eyes began to fill with tears. The apples were green and hard, but the laughter was even harder.

The children now threw away all restraint. They formed a circle around the tree and sent apples buzzing at their target. I could find none to throw; those that scored either bounced back or were snatched up by someone behind me. Finally I found one, which I hurled at one of the shadows. It missed. The laughter was harder still.

I was overcome by misery and fury. At last I flung my arms up to protect my face and charged wildly at my tormentors. With shouts of delight they danced and skipped out of my way like dry leaves before an autumn wind. Pursuit was hopeless. I was at their mercy and they had no mercy.

In one of my hopeless charges I hit the tree, fell to my knees, and the tears came. Struggling to my feet, I launched one last desperate attack. This time one of the girls let herself be caught. She stood perfectly still, making no effort to resist.

"Just what are you going to do? What do you think you can do?" she asked.

God! What could I do? Nothing. Nothing. They had laughed, jeered, and tormented me because I could not see. Even if I could beat them all, revenge would erase nothing.

A screen door creaked.

"Children," came a voice from the house, "I don't want any fighting, do you hear? If you can't play nicely, you'll have to go somewhere else. Ellie, I've just taken some cookies out of the oven. Come in and you can have one with your milk. The rest of you go on home."

Still excited, the children giggled as they happily scampered off.

This was my tree of knowledge whose fruit I had not eaten, but whose bitterness I had tasted. I left my Eden for the land of the white crow.

3. Catching Angels

My father and mother had an uncommon amount of natural wisdom. They gave me then, and for the rest of their lives, all the love and understanding parents can give to a child. They never protected me because of my blindness. They never prevented me from doing all the things ordinary children do, and therefore *they* never made me unduly conscious that I was different. They neither prodded nor cautioned me. They had no idea of what I could or could not do, and neither did I; but they had the great good sense to let me find out for myself.

In their relationship with each other, they showed they understood the secret of love: freedom. They never demanded anything of each other as a matter of right, so each gave all to the other freely. Loving their children, they did not interfere with their lives.

The temptation to interfere with mine, though, must have been very strong. I had to go to school, but where? They could enter me in the local system or ship me off to one of the two state institutes for the blind, one in up-state New York and one in New York City. Though I might have found the local public school confusing, they would have been there to help and comfort me each night. This was the temptation set by love that they resisted for my sake. Even though it would mean the repeated wrench of long separations, they were convinced it would be best for me to go to a special school, with its special equipment and special teachers. After investigating both institutes, they decided the school in upstate New York was more vocational than academic and felt that the academic training would, in the long run, be better.

The New York Institute is situated in what was then a thinly populated section of the Bronx not far from the zoo. Its fourteen-acre campus was surrounded by a seven-foot steel fence. The campus was an oblong divided into thirds by imaginary lines running across it. The first third was given over to the Lower School, grades one through three; the other two housed the students in grades four through twelve. This larger section was divided by a line separating the girls from the boys.

The Lower School consisted of one main building in which the children were housed, fed, and taught. Both the building and the grounds surrounding it were also

sliced in two—a girls' side and a boys' side. The classrooms occupied the first floor, with the dining rooms in
the center. In the basement was a small gymnasium. The
bedrooms, each containing six beds and six lockers, were
on the second floor.

Amid the acrid smell of metal polish and disinfect-
ant, my mother unpacked my suitcase.

My first week end at school was momentous. Saturday
it rained. About eight of us were cooped up all morning
in a large room down in the basement. Toward noon,
time began to hang heavy, and one of the boys, John, became especially bored. Since I was a new boy and small
into the bargain, it was only natural that he should
launch an attack on me. I was then thin and weak from
my year of sickness, and no match for him.

My beating was proceeding in a workmanlike fashion
when Kenneth and Anthony interfered. They saved my
life—or so I thought—and, as they picked me up and
comforted me, we swore eternal friendship. I went up to
lunch that day with a warm glow inside. I had two
friends. What was even more exciting, I had a real live
enemy.

After this, I was a new boy no longer, and I adjusted
easily to the Institute's routine.

We were wakened every morning at six by a bell,
snatched our towels from our lockers, and dashed down
the hall to the showers. After the showers, which always
ended with thirty seconds of ice water, we ran back to
our rooms to dress. This was a very exciting time of day,
a time for playing tag, for pillow and towel fights.

When the next bell rang, we were shooed outside for

twenty minutes of fresh air before breakfast. At ten past
seven we were ravenously hungry, and I never refused
anything.

After breakfast we returned to our rooms, made our
beds, and then did as we pleased until another bell summoned us to assembly at ten after eight. We read a Psalm,
sang a hymn, and listened to a few general admonitions
to the effect that we ought to be good children, shouldn't
pinch our neighbors, and should sit up straight. Then
we were sent off to class.

I began learning how to read Braille in the first grade.
It was very simple to learn, probably because I was not
really certain about the print alphabet and therefore had
nothing much to forget. By the end of six weeks I had
learned to read simple sentences.

Braille has been elevated to the realm of the occult by
those who know nothing about it. People have always
either marveled at or ignored things they don't understand, so it is really not surprising that they should dissolve in admiration before someone purporting to make
sense out of a sheet of paper covered with pimples. Reading and writing Braille can be learned easily by a sighted
person. As soon as I went off to school, my mother
learned it and wrote me letters long before I could read
well enough to understand them. I don't mean to mini-
mize my mother's achievement, for though it is relatively
easy to learn how to read Braille, it is far more arduous
to write it.

In the first grade I was unimpressed with Braille—Nature Study was far more interesting. Half the library of
the Lower School was devoted to stuffed animals and

birds. Miss Miller, our first-grade teacher, used to bring a few of them into class every day and we all crowded around her table and ran our fingers over them while she told us stories about them. One day she produced a porcupine.

"Now, children," she said, "you must all be very, very careful. The porcupine is like a little pig with lots of sharp needles sticking out of him."

She took our hands and carefully ran them down the porcupine's back from head to tail. Johnnie Morris, a boy with a good deal of sight, was assisting by doing the same thing for some of the other children who could see nothing. He was showing me the porcupine's tail and guiding my hand along by holding my wrist, when he suddenly gave it a sharp push upward so that I squeaked with pain. I bit the quills out of my fingers, but not the pain. Five minutes later I had recovered sufficiently to do the same thing to the next boy, Anthony Ackerman. Miss Miller was slightly deaf, but Anthony yelled louder than I had, so she heard, investigated, and caught us literally red-handed.

Miss Miller must have been an amateur naturalist, for she loved animals and succeeded in communicating that love to me. When she put a bluebird into my hands she was trying to give me a part of the world.

Among the stories of H. G. Wells is one called "The Country of the Blind." It describes the adventures of a sighted person who stumbles into a valley whose inhabitants cannot see. They think the air is alive with singing angels. Because they can always hear, but never see the birds, and because they can never catch one to examine it, they build legends about these phantoms that exist outside their perceivable universe.

A strange sound in the night—not necessarily frightening; perhaps even lovely; but nevertheless a sound that demands its mystery be fathomed, drawing us to the edge of the known: where does it come from? What makes it? Thus, in *The Tempest,* Ferdinand, finding himself in a strange new world, is drawn irresistibly onward by the sweet music of the invisible Ariel:

> "Where should this music be? i' th' air or th' earth?
> It sounds no more;—And sure, it waits upon
> Some god o' th' island. Sitting on a bank,
> Weeping again the king my father's wrack,
> This music crept by me upon the waters,
> Allaying both their fury, and my passion,
> With its sweet air: thence I have follow'd it,—
> Or it hath drawn me rather—but 'tis gone.
> No, it begins again.
>   *(Ariel sings)*
> Full fathom five thy father lies;
>   Of his bones are coral made:
> Those are pearls that were his eyes:
>   Nothing of him that doth fade,
> But doth suffer a sea-change
> Into something rich and strange.
> Sea-nymphs hourly ring his knell:
>   *[Burden:* Ding-dong.]
> Hark! Now I hear them,—ding-dong, bell."

Like Ferdinand, we follow our music. We seek out the cricket or the creaking board in the night, and so it is with my birds.

That is why I have longed to have a robin, a cardinal, or a mockingbird. I long to tame him so he will perch upon my finger, so I can touch him, so I shall understand where the music comes from and what it is that makes the dark house of my world a place of miracles.

So, also, the chemist or the physicist hears the music of the molecules. He cages them and feels the mounting pressure of joy that comes with growing understanding. I felt this too, when a canary first set a tentative toe on my extended finger.

To my great delight, our class was divided into four tables: the Bluebirds, the Robins, the Butterflies, and the Bunnies. The Bluebirds were the cleverest, the Robins next, the Butterflies were quite undependable, and the Bunnies paid only a pale tribute in lip service to lessons. They spent most of their time larking. My obvious pleasure in Miss Miller's animal stories led her to seat me with the Bluebirds, though I confess to a few visits to the Robins. I had to give up my honored seat at the Bluebirds' table whenever Miss Miller caught me sitting astride instead of upon my chair in the normal way. The first time, it was quite by accident that I was sitting with one leg on either side of the chair and my feet curled about the front legs.

"Robert," cried Miss Miller as she gave my ear a tug, "sit around there properly. Anyone would think you were riding a horse instead of sitting on a chair."

"Riding a horse!" I thought. "What a wonderful idea!" And thereafter I surreptitiously covered many miles of lonely prairie on my trusty bronco, and I also spent a good deal of time with the Robins.

But my sins were small. I conformed. However, I looked with a mixture of admiration and awe at Peter, a boy who could and did imitate a police siren every morning on his way to the showers. Peter was a pillar of the Bunnies' table. He was a notorious rowdy who, instead of asking to be excused, as often as not answered that frequent demand of nature in the corner behind the plant stand. The public humiliation that always followed hard upon discovery never in the least dampened his vitality and good humor. He and I were great chums, admiring each other extravagantly—or, rather, I admired him extravagantly. There, but for the lack of courage, went I.

After morning classes we all had fifteen minutes in which to wash for lunch; at 12:15 everyone went to his room, got his towel, went down the hall to wash, and then back to his room again.

In my third and last year in the Lower School, one of my roommates was that same John who had given me my first sound thrashing. John and I always raced to see who could get to our room first. The race was more than a test of speed; it was a jockeying for position. If I got there first, I hid under the bed. When John came in for his towel, I leaped on him and the battle was on. But it was really unfair because I never knew when I was first. If he had reached the room first he would stand quietly watching me as I dropped to my knees to crawl under a bed. Then, with a "Now I've got you, you little rat!" he would fling

himself upon me. If he didn't feel like fighting, he simply waited in the hall until time forced me to take my
towel and run down to wash. Then he would take his,
and, for all I knew, wash at the very next basin.

We had both long since forgotten the original grudge,
if there ever had been one, that started our first fight.
So just to have our minds easy on the score of provoca-
tion, we used to preface our daily matches with a fresh
insult or two if we thought about it. If we forgot, or if
there wasn't any time, we never let this stand between
us and our pleasure.

The bell for lunch proclaimed our truce. If we had
not yet washed, we did so hurriedly and, flushed with
exertion and excitement, ran down to the dining room
together. A fresh bruise or a red nose often brought
pointed questions from the teachers who sat at our
tables. But honor demanded silence, and we always honored honor.

Everyone wanted to sit at the table presided over by
Miss McMurray, our third-grade teacher, for we all
loved her. She came from the West. The West was the
home of Smoky, Big Enough, and all the other Will
James characters. I secretly hoped Miss McMurray kept
a horse in her room and that some morning she would
come galloping down the hall to assembly. I was her
willing slave and did my arithmetic quickly so I could
sit and dream of her.

She taught us how to knit, too, and though I strove to
master the art for her sake, I was forever pricking my
fingers, dropping stitches, and getting myself and my
yarn into magnificent tangles. This had its advantages,

however, because it forced her to spend long minutes with me untangling, catching up my stitches, and alternately scolding and comforting. I actually did finish a marble bag that year.

I was so proud of my handiwork that it did not seem right to use it for marbles. It was so lovely it was fit for only one purpose: I tied a long piece of cord to the drawstrings of the bag and hung it out of my bedroom window. Perhaps a robin in search of a home would find it and move in. Then I planned to creep from my bed in the darkness of night, give the string a quick jerk, and haul in my angel.

4. Misfits

Unfortunately, my scheme failed. The principal saw the bag hanging out of my window and demanded it be removed.

Naturally, none of us was supposed to like the principal—that was understood among us. He was a malevolent deity on a far mountaintop, but the wrath of his rod seldom interfered with the quiet routine of our lives. He had nothing to do with my view of the place.

In fact, superficially I got on very well. I liked my teachers, made good grades, found a wide assortment of friends, and had a respectable number of fights. On one level, I could have been described as a "well-adjusted child." Part of me *was* well adjusted, but there was another part that was *not*. This other self was not in rebellion; it was simply separate, distinct, private.

This part was antisocial. It would not go to the Lower School at 999 Pelham Parkway and sit calmly behind the steel fence surrounding the campus. It maintained its integrity by refusing to accept the pleasures of conforming. It saved its energies for voyages off into the mountains and to the North Woods during the recess periods in the afternoons.

I wandered about the grounds by myself, playing my private games, climbing mountains and fighting battles-to-the-death—all of which I won—with animals Thornton Burgess never even dreamed of; and all the while my hearing was growing more and more acute. I could follow a leaf or a bit of paper as it skittered along the drive, and I knew when and how far to jump so as to land directly upon it. I was learning to judge direction and distance very precisely by sound alone.

I was good at seeing with my ears, but not remarkable. At playing ball and doing other things requiring very good hearing, I was among the best in the school, but I was not *the* best.

How can one's ears tell the precise direction as well as the distance between oneself and, say, a tree?

Like this: The sound of one's footsteps returns as an echo, having bounced back from the tree. But the echo is heard by the right ear sooner than by the left because the left ear is farther from the tree than the right. All that needs to be done is to turn the head until the echo reaches both ears at the same time, and then one is facing the tree. But, of course, it isn't necessary to face the tree. The brain automatically takes the fraction of silence between the time the right ear hears and the time the left ear hears, and, by interpreting this lapse in terms of the speed of sound, can judge the way the head must be turned.

Distance is another matter. The standard unit of measurement is the distance between the heel and the ears. The nerves running from my heels to my brain tell me instantly when my foot hits the sidewalk. A fraction of a second elapses before my ears confirm this fact. After walking around for a few years listening to one's own footsteps, one's brain becomes accustomed to the fact that the lapse of time between setting down the foot and hearing the footstep means it has taken sound that long to travel the height of the body. With this unit as the measure, I can easily judge the distance between myself and a tree by dividing by two the time it takes me to hear the echo from the tree and comparing this with the time it takes to hear my own footstep.

I developed this capacity for locating sounds on a broad concrete walk that extended the whole length of the campus and passed very near the Lower School. For some strange reason the authorities had placed rocks about the size of large footstools at irregular intervals along either side of the walk. These rocks caused many a bruised shin and scraped knee, but I liked them nevertheless. They reminded me of the mountains and rocky ravines where Buster, the big brown bear, waged his endless war against Loop, the lynx. I climbed on these rocks and crouched there growling to myself, waiting for a lynx to pass.

I waited there on my boulder for a gust of wind to blow a dry leaf or a scrap of paper along the concrete; then, snarling ferociously—more like a lynx than a bear, I'm afraid—I leaped upon my feline prey and invariably demolished him with a crushing blow from my powerful right paw. Buster was my hero. I thought much more about him than I did about either Babe Ruth or Lindbergh. Though I had nothing against anyone who hit sixty home runs in a season or who flew across the Atlantic alone, it was, on the whole, much more satisfying to be a bear.

A bear was free.

Beyond the walk was the seven-foot steel fence encircling the Institute. I knew the sound of every one of the gates in that fence, and the clang of a gate always excited my imagination and curiosity. Was someone coming in? Was someone going out? Where was that someone going? I would listen to hear whether footsteps came upon the walk to the building or whether they just faded away.

On week ends we took long walks with Mrs. Cummings, the boys' housemother. When the gate slammed shut behind us I could even taste the freedom. On that first night in September of 1931 when my mother had unpacked my suitcase in the room reeking with the sharp smell of polished metal, I had made up my mind. There was one thing I wanted—one above all others: I wanted to walk out of that gate, never to return. Meanwhile, I solaced myself with the weekly taste of the untainted air outside.

Mrs. Cummings, herself a newcomer to New York, took us to the Bronx Zoo, up to City Island, and we had more than one picnic on the shores of Pelham Bay.

This was great fun—not because I was thrilled at seeing a tiger or at gazing out over the waves of the bay, for I never saw either the tiger or the bay. I smelled the tiger. The smell is the part most people find distasteful about a zoo, but it filled me with shivers of excitement. Also, I heard the tiger crunch a bone. For me, a tiger is the splintering power of those jaws, not the yellow velvet of his coat.

Unless things have changed, Pelham Bay is not renowned for its scenic beauty. But its ugliness, if it was ugly, never came between it and me. The fresh salt breeze blowing from the ocean brought to me over the mud flats and littered shore all the mystery of the sea. These sounds and smells filled me with a strange, tense excitement; they were the sounds and smells of freedom.

My quarrel was not with the school or the people who ran it or the people who taught me. My quarrel was with the fence. The first week I spent behind it, I beat it with my fists until my knuckles bled. Thank God for Mrs. Cummings and those long walks in the sweet air outside.

She was particularly kind to me because I was so frail and so far from home. Most of the other children were from the metropolitan area and their parents came every Friday afternoon to take them home for the week end. I could go only at Christmas, Easter, and for the summer. For most of the pleasures of those week ends I have Mrs. Cummings to thank. She was wonderful in so many ways, and, of course, none of us really appreciated her.

She was responsible, too, for many a happy evening. Almost every night she read to us for at least an hour, and there was always an outcry when she shut the book and sent us off to bed. Back home at 13 Edward Street we had an attic full of children's books, and I used to return from every vacation laden with new Tarzans, *The Swiss Family Robinson,* and always a liberal supply of James Oliver Curwood, who, for years, was my favorite.

When we were excused from the supper table, we scrambled upstairs to the sitting room and fought for places close to the chair we knew Mrs. Cummings always sat in. We even turned off Chandu the Magician when Mrs. Cummings offered to read before supper as well. We were all devoted slaves of Chandu, and I'm sure the others hoped, as I did, to grow up one day and marry Little Orphan Annie. But when the chips were down, when we had to choose between *Tom Sawyer* and any one of the radio serials, *Tom Sawyer* and Mrs. Cummings invariably won.

As my third year in New York drew to a close, my heart was sore. In the fall, I was to return not to the Lower School, but to the Upper School and the fourth grade. I did not want to leave Mrs. Cummings and Miss McMurray. Although I had no love for the Lower School, it was a tiny world in which I felt secure. I knew the playground, my schoolfellows, the teachers, and the daily schedule; I knew what was expected of me at every turn, and I knew how to perform it. What could I possibly gain by leaving it? I would have to learn all over again everything I had already learned. For the first few weeks every step would be a step into the unknown. I would have to navigate among strange rocks, pillars, fire hydrants, swings, walls, and doors; I would have to learn the exact position of every hazard before I could rest easy even about geography. I looked forward to all this with no more enthusiasm than I imagine a crab feels at the prospect of having to dispense with its old shell.

In order to grow, a crab has to discard his old shell with its familiar comforts, and until he succeeds in creating a new one he is extremely vulnerable. His life is the story of his passage through successive shells until he succeeds too well. He makes one so strong that he cannot escape from it, and he dies.

Though having to leave the Lower School was painful, it was perhaps easier for me than for some of my friends. I was already practiced in departure. The wisdom of my parents had broken for me the magic circle of 13 Edward Street.

Some of the other children were not so fortunate. For example, there was Freddy. Like all of us, Freddy hated being forced from the comfort and security of his home, but he was more sensitive than I, for he seemed unable to recover from the experience. It was harder for him because the pain was repeated every Sunday evening. He lived in the city, so he spent each week end in the bosom of his most loving family.

When they picked him up on Friday afternoon he wept with joy, and when they brought him back on Sunday evening he wept with misery. Then they spent at least half an hour preparing him for their departure. Taking him to a corner of our lounge, his mother whispered sweet promises about the coming week end. Meanwhile, Freddy wept almost silently. A quaver crept into his mother's voice. She blew her nose, whispered a reminder about his prayers, kissed him again, tried to leave, turned at the doorway, then rushed back to sweep him into her arms, a quivering, blubbering mass of misery.

When she finally tore herself from him one Sunday evening, she stood quietly crying in the hall until she intercepted one of the school's bullies:

"Hello, Charlie," she called softly, trying to sound pleased to see him. "Will you come outside with me for a moment? I'm Freddy's mother." Expecting the worst, the boy went sullenly along behind her.

"Now then, Charlie," as she caught her breath and blew her nose again, "I know you like candy." She fumbled in her purse, "so I've brought you . . . brought you . . . a dollar to buy candy with," and she crumpled the bill into the boy's limp hand. "Now this is a sort of bargain, Charlie, do you see? Freddy . . . Freddy isn't very strong and he gets frightened easily. It's silly, isn't it, but he does. He says he gets lost, too. Sometimes he can't find his way to the dining room, and he keeps losing his towel, he says. You'll help him, won't you? I'm sure a fine big boy like you would help a boy like Freddy." And, squeezing Charlie's half-closed hand and catching her breath again, she hurried away without waiting for his answer. She knew Charlie did not want the dollar. He liked candy, but he didn't like being bought off from his more regular pleasures. And even if Charlie consented to being bribed, there were all the other boys. Suppose she could buy off the whole school—Freddy would still mislay his towel, lose himself on the playground, and be desperately afraid.

Charlie was only a drop in the bucket of Freddy's misery. We plagued him. Even if we had treated him with affection and tenderness, which is outlawed among boys, life for him at the Institute would still have been purgatory. But we made it absolute hell. We never beat him up—it wasn't worth the effort; he was too weak. I don't believe any of us ever gave him even an intentional push. We despised him too much. We confined ourselves to jeering. He was a living symbol of all our weaknesses, he was our scapegoat, and instead of abusing ourselves, we abused him.

One day Freddy did not turn up at his table for lunch. Mrs. Cummings went out to look for him. In a few minutes she came back and asked some of the teachers to help her. An hour later they found him, wedged into his own locker, his mouth stuffed with handkerchiefs and a towel wound tightly about his head.

"What is it?" cried Mrs. Cummings. "What happened, Freddy? Tell me!"

"Nothing . . . nothing happened," Freddy sobbed.

"What do you mean, nothing? How did you . . . who did this to you?"

"I did it myself," he moaned.

"Why, what are you talking about? Why on earth . . . ?"

"Because I thought I could do it that way. I thought I could kill myself."

After that, we left him pretty much alone.

5. Blind Man's Buff

When I entered school, I weighed forty pounds, but the regular hours, good food, and fresh air had done their work. When I left the Lower School, I must have looked rather like a half barrel of beer set up on two piano legs.

The Upper School had a large athletic field that was perfect for football. The janitor of the Lower School had given me plenty of instruction about how a football should be kicked, and I was an apt scholar. Consequently, when I heard the thud of a football on my first evening in the Upper School, I rushed out onto the field. The ball landed near me on the grass, so I chased it.

"Hey, give us the ball, kid," cried a strange voice.

Obediently I carried the ball and pushed it into the

stomach of the player who had called. The big boy patted me on the shoulder.

"Thanks. Are you a new kid? What's your name? Can you kick?"

"Sure," I replied, and, taking the ball, I gave it a resounding boot.

The ball sailed far out into the field and I went dashing after it, because I knew that, while kicking was important, being able to field was even more so. The secret of finding a ball is to catch up with it before it stops rolling, for there is nothing quieter than a dead ball. I caught up with my kick, grabbed the ball, and gave it a lusty kick back to the fellow. I heard him say to another boy, "You hear that kick? It's only a kid. Jeez, he can kick as well as I can. A fat little guy, just like a turkey. Hey, Turkey, you want to play after study hour? You're on my team."

I had started off on the right foot. I would fit in here or, at least, part of me would.

Our brand of football was called "kicking goals." After teams were chosen, we went out onto the field, which was about seventy-five yards square. One team protected the cement walk behind one of the dormitories, and the other guarded the drive that ran along next to the steel fence forming the campus boundary. Each team took up its position about twenty yards in front of its own goal. The first kicker took the ball and shouted, "Ready?" When he heard, "Okay, shsh! you guys," the kicker stepped forward and *boom!* the game was on.

Each team had to kick from where one of its members

had touched the ball, so there was always a mad scramble to touch it before it stopped rolling. The unpredictable way a football bounces makes chasing it by a team of blind boys violent and exciting. There was never any intentional tackling in our game—very little, anyway; and it was never openly recognized as a vital part of the game. There were always collisions, and the air was usually dark with purple oaths as the whole team stumbled over one another frantically trying to reach the ball before it stopped bouncing. There was a good reason for having cement walks as goals. The whack of a leather ball landing on cement is public evidence of success.

We cheated whenever we could. When we picked up the ball, we could be fairly certain no one on the other side would know whether we kicked it from exactly that point or whether we brought it forward just a step or two. But ears are almost as good as eyes under certain circumstances.

"Ready?" the voice would call.

"No, get back there. I heard you." The kicker would then stamp his feet as though retreating to his proper position and call in a slightly weaker voice, "Ready?" "Yeah, okay; that's better."

Boom would go the kick, usually accompanied by a "There! you blind bastards!" This affectionately contemptuous way of referring to our blindness was universal among us.

There were other games, too, such as baseball. We played it in what we called "The Court," a paved rectangle about forty-five feet long and eighteen feet wide enclosed on three sides by buildings. The windows of the dormitories opening onto this court were all covered by heavy steel gratings, a wise precaution.

The batter, with a sawed-off broomstick in his hand, stood at one end of The Court and lined himself up with the long wall on his right. The pitcher stood about halfway down, facing the batter, lining himself up by the same wall on his left. We used an ordinary child's rubber ball about five inches in diameter. The pitcher would say, "Ready?"

"Okay."

The pitcher threw the ball so it bounced just once before it reached the batter, and the batter judged from the sound of the bounce the ball's height and speed, and swung accordingly. He had three swings. We had no umpires. Those of us without sight would never accept the decisions of anyone who had a little. Whenever somebody took upon himself the duties of an umpire, his calls of "ball" or "strike" were shouted down.

"Shut up, will you?" the batter would cry. "You're as blind as a bat. Hell, you can't see any better than I can." This defiance always won support from the batter's team, and the self-appointed umpire usually had to beat a hasty retreat for his own safety.

Our fielding, needless to say, was never up to much, but our lack of skill was compensated for by the size of The Court. With six or seven fielders rushing madly about, pushing and jostling one another, the batter made only slow progress toward first base. The game was as turbulent as football.

There were four boys' dormitories or "houses" in

the Upper School, each of which had five or six rooms with six boys in each. One's teammates were usually also roommates and each room seemed to have its own particular characteristics. Some played games while others didn't. I was always with ball players. Generally speaking, each room went into things pretty much as one man. There were always some rooms that were hard for the housemother to control, while others never gave her any trouble at all.

To help the housemother, each house had a male proctor; he lived a dog's life. Every night at ten o'clock he came around to make certain we were all quiet. He must have spent most of his nights standing in the hall with an ear glued to keyholes to catch the slightest whisper. Probably he had been issued felt-soled shoes when he signed his contract, for he could move up and down those halls with treacherous silence. More than once our door flew open and a deep voice would growl, "All right, now! Another word out of this room and you'll all stand in the hall for an hour, and we'll see how you like that!"

On rare occasions when the proctor could not manage us—for there were times when even he found it difficult to be in more than one place at a time—the housemother, full of indignation, would issue from her room bent on mayhem.

One of our proctors, a German refugee Doctor of Philosophy named Schmidt, was a man full of childlike enthusiasm as well as deep thoughts, and he entered into our games with as much relish as we did. But sometimes his zest carried him across the boundary line between student and teacher.

One night when the learned doctor came in to quiet us at ten o'clock, we ambushed him and carried him to a bed where we tickled him mercilessly. Above his shouts of laughter one of us heard the slam of the housemother's door and the quick hissing shuffle of slippered feet approaching like angry serpents.

"Hey! Chickie!" and the hoarse whisper cut short our merriment like a guillotine. Everyone dashed for his bed, leaped in, and fought to control his delight at the approaching crisis. The boy on whose bed Dr. Schmidt lay had nowhere to go; so, with admirable presence of mind, he tried to cover the victim with a spread while he himself crawled beneath the bed. When the housemother turned on the light, every bed would be occupied and we and the doctor might escape with only a tongue-lashing.

All might have gone well had not Schmidt lost his nerve. Just before the serpent reached our door, he sprang from the bed and dived for a corner beside the row of steel lockers. He hit them with a tremendous crash but he tucked himself into the tiny space as best he could. The boy under the empty bed realized that this rash act forced him into the open, and he was crawling out to climb into the bed when the door was flung open, the light snapped on, and an angry voice called, "Now, just what's going on here? What do you think you're doing there? Get into bed! Who made all that noise with the lockers, eh? Who did it? Speak up, now!"

She evidently sensed that something was afoot more mysterious than a boy's crawling on the floor, so she entered the room and looked around suspiciously. She caught sight of the renowned doctor crouching in the corner and, not recognizing him at first, she cried, "All right, you! Come right out of there! What do you think you're doing, anyway? Get right back to . . . Well! . . . Say! . . . Yes . . . I see." And her anger trailed off into confusion.

The wonderful thing about the incident was that all the boys got off scot free. She couldn't have made us stand in the hall without also insisting that Schmidt stand there too. I hope he was not reproved by the administration, because he was the innocent victim of an ambush, and of the six who had attacked him, four were on the varsity wrestling team.

I started wrestling about a year after coming to the Upper School. Clyde Downs, our athletic coach, thought he could see a potential wrestler beneath the fat and behind my fears. If, over a period of two or three years, he could pare off the fat and inspire me with confidence, he might have something for the varsity. He looked on all of us as potential athletes, and to him being an athlete meant being first of all a man. He felt his job to lie more with the mind than with the body.

His methods were not subtle. At the beginning of each gym period we had to run a quarter of a mile, or six laps around the oval track that encircled the gymnasium like a gallery. There were railings on either side of the track, and with our left hands resting on the inside rail, we dashed around; or, rather, the rest dashed while I chugged.

Getting around once seemed to me an impossible demand to make of my short fat legs, and as for six times, that was ridiculous. Mr. Downs assigned big strong boys as herdsmen on sluggards like me, and they were given carte blanche. One came thundering up behind me.

"Go on past," I urged, "I'll wait!"

"Hurry up!" the tormentor snapped as he jabbed a fist in my ribs. I didn't dare stop to fight or even complain, because I would certainly be run down by the crowd. If anyone ever did stop, he was not only run down accidentally but he was picked up and then deliberately knocked down for having been so stupid as to stop.

Shaking, gasping, and with a stitch in one side from the exertion and a stitch in the other side from the herdsman's fist, I staggered through the door, lied to the sentry about the number of laps I had run, and stumbled down the stairs. I groped my way to a corner and collapsed.

The gymnasium always seethed with tumult. Wrestlers rolled and thumped on the mats, and bouncing basketballs punctuated the echoing thunder on the track. It seemed to me madness to venture out into this maelstrom. The obvious thing to do was to creep into a corner, make myself as small as possible, and hope no one would fall over me. When Mr. Downs blew the whistle to begin the class, it would be safe to come out.

One day I lay quivering with exhaustion in my corner, waiting for the whistle and grateful for a few moments of peace, when suddenly *Whack!* a basketball bounced off the wall just above me. My heart skipped a beat. That was a close one! Then *whack!* again, and again. I crept along the wall to escape from the target, but the ball followed me. Finally I shouted: "Hey, cut it out, will you!"

Thud! the leather ball struck me heavily on the shoulder. I leaned back against the wall and began to whimper. *Bang!* An even heavier blow smashed into my face.

"Hey, Russell," called Mr. Downs sharply, "get out of there; you'll get hurt like that. Get out here on the mats and do something."

The next afternoon when I staggered down from the track and sank against the wall, again the big, hard basketball slammed into the paneling beside my head. Shaking with rage and terror, I struggled to my feet and rushed at my tormentor in that chaos of sound. I didn't catch him. I was still choking with anguish when, ten minutes later, Mr. Downs gave me a big boy to wrestle. My anger poured out on my adversary. Mr. Downs was delighted to see me so furious and at that moment decided I was probably worth working on. The following year I made the Junior Varsity as a 125-pounder.

I had my first match when we met the School for the Deaf up in White Plains. Long before we reached White Plains I was terrified. When my turn came, I made it as far as the middle of the mats, where my opponent grasped my right hand in a powerful greeting. The referee gave us our instructions and the battle was on. I had not minded fighting with John back in the third grade; I did not even mind wrestling with the other boys on our own squad; but to get out on the mats in a strange place in front of a big crowd to fight with someone whom I had never even met—at the age of ten this was too much. I was pinned in about one minute. I hope, for honor's sake, that I struggled, but I suspect I really fainted.

I won the next match, but not because of any heroic determination. I fought because I was afraid.

The next year I was eleven, and I had the misfortune to make the varsity. After the elimination bouts were over and the varsity positions had been decided for our first meet, Mr. Downs called all the wrestlers together.

"Fellows," he began, "you all know I've always wanted the team to compete with ordinary schools as well as schools for the handicapped. It's not easy to get them to agree to wrestle a school like us. After all, look at it from their point of view. If they beat us, well, they're supposed to. No one deserves any credit for beating a bunch of blind boys. If we beat them, why, they're disgraced; so they don't have much to gain.

"Still, I've managed to get something really exciting for our first meet this Saturday. It's your big chance, boys. Hold on to your seats, now. We're going to wrestle the Junior Varsity of Columbia University!"

"Holy smokes!" somebody muttered after a short silence.

"My God!" I thought. I was then just entering the sixth grade. Maybe I would get sick in time.

But everything failed me, and Saturday afternoon at about four o'clock in the Columbia gym I found myself quivering on the bench. George, our 115-pounder, was first. He was a beautiful wrestler and didn't care whom he beat. The Columbia man was looking at the ceiling in three minutes, and George was being pounded on the back by everybody except me. With icy fingers I began weakly tugging at my heavy sweat shirt.

"Come on, now, Fat Stuff!" laughed Mr. Downs happily, "let's have another just like the last one!"

"Yeah, Russ, you give it to him! You show him!" called the other fellows on the bench. George sat down beside me, breathing easily.

"How was it, George?" I stammered.

"Easy; just go out and give him hell."

"What's the matter, Fat? Come on," said Mr. Downs.

"I can't get my sweat shirt off." A big hand ripped the shirt from my back in one movement, and another big hand planted firmly between my shoulders drove me out onto the mats.

"Don't push!" I objected. "I'm going; I'm going!"

"Over here!" called the referee. I pretended to be confused, but he came over and got me. "All right, now; you fellows both know the rules, I guess."

"Sure!" growled a deep voice.

"Well," I said, "I'm not . . ." but he paid no attention to my muttering.

"All right; now, let's have a good match. Go to your corners . . . Ready! *Wrestle!*" I listened intently for the sound of my opponent's footsteps. There they were! The footsteps of a college man, and coming right after *me!* I would have collapsed, but two powerful clamps gripped my arms. I leaned forward. My adversary bobbed and swayed easily. He was loose, powerful, and agile. I was almost paralyzed. Suddenly he dropped to his knees, grabbed both my ankles, and I was flat on my back. He was so surprised by my cooperation that I had time to roll over and do my best to simulate a turtle. He seemed untroubled by this. I "opened up" when he inadvertently rubbed my shoulder with his cheek. He hadn't shaved that morning, and the fact that my opponent had an actual beard utterly defeated me. I reached out to push him off; he grabbed my arm, whipped me over, and the referee thumped the mats.

In spite of my shameful exhibition, we trounced the Columbia team and continued to do so for several years. But I had put up such an awful showing that Mr. Downs decided I had to be spoken to. The following Monday he summoned me into his office.

"Well, what have you got to say for yourself?" he asked solemnly.

"Nothing," I said uneasily.

"You were a pushover. Do you know that?"

I knew that; I had been thinking about it all week end. I had decided that the prestige of being on the wrestling team just wasn't worth the misery of having to wrestle strange people, and certainly not college men.

"I'm quitting," I said.

He paused for a moment to consider his attack.

"Do you know what the fellows say about you?" He waited for an answer, but I would give none. "They say you've got a streak down your back—a yellow streak. They say you're a coward. Are you going to let them say that?"

"I quit," I repeated stolidly.

As the year passed, I had plenty of regrets about being just a private citizen; however, I kept them to myself.

But Mr. Downs wouldn't leave me alone. The following year he baited a hook and one day during our regular gym class he announced that some of the wrestlers guaranteed they could pin the following—and he read out a list of names. I was one of "the following." I didn't have any choice as to whether I would wrestle the varsity man; I had to do it. What everybody wanted to see was whether he could pin me as he had said he could. He didn't. I pinned him. Mr. Downs saw I was drunk with victory, so he placed a few well-chosen compliments in my ear and again I was his boy.

I still had my old trouble, though. I could beat fellows from school, but I couldn't pin a sack of flour from another school. However, and this was some improvement, they couldn't pin me. I developed an expert defense.

I didn't really gain full confidence until I was about fourteen. The wrestling coach from City College sent our team an open invitation to come down on Saturday mornings for workouts. After the first Saturday with strangers, I was all right. Because there were none of the formalities of a match, I found I could beat one of them —then two—then three. . . . From that point on, I was undefeated in team competition.

Our team wrestled schools in Philadelphia and Baltimore. On one trip we stopped for dinner in Trenton, New Jersey. Our captain, Bob Rossiter, ordered turkey and happened to pick up on his fork the small paper cup holding the cranberry sauce. Bob had excellent manners and knew he shouldn't return anything to his plate, especially in public, so he contented himself with chewing thoughtfully on the wad of paper and, after tucking it away in his cheek, managed to go on with the meal on three cylinders.

The waitress, however, had seen him pop the paper cup into his mouth and the experience shook her severely. She lost control of herself and dissolved in tears of pity for the poor blind boy who couldn't tell the difference between turkey and a paper cup. The coach, who enjoyed such things enormously and who had seen what the waitress had seen, told us about her after we got back on the bus. We whooped with laughter all the way to Baltimore.

Mr. Downs was an excellent coach and he trained some really first-rate wrestlers, but he was much more important as a molder of character and attitude. He did everything he could to make people like me aggressive, and he took the edge off those who thought they were invincible. Clyde Downs was one of the few people at the Institute who worked creatively with our psychological problems. He taught us that we could win in competition with the sighted.

6. Saturday Review

I had managed to grow a new shell in the Upper School, and while there was no Mrs. Cummings or Miss McMurray, there were other and even better things—the football, baseball, wrestling, and dark plots against the proctors. Above all was the increasing sense of comradeship. But around even the sweetest of these pleasures was that terrible fence in whose shadow even the greatest joy left a bitter taste. In those earlier years at my solitary games I had listened to the clanging of the steel gates. To breathe freedom outside had been my dream, and now in the Upper School this dream came true, at least on week ends.

When a student was twelve years old, his parents could

sign a slip releasing the school from all responsibility in case of accident, and the happy boy could have week-end passes. Permissions were granted until ten o'clock on Friday and Saturday evenings and until nine on Sundays.

With trembling hands I took my first slip from the principal's office to my housemother and made a dash for the gate. I had nowhere to go; but to stand outside the fence was enough.

To be truthful, I was afraid to go anywhere by myself. This was all new territory: I did not know the curbs, the trees, or the streets.

Fortunately, there was another boy in the same predica-ment. Together we mustered the courage to explore the wilderness of the Bronx. Stumbling over curbs and run-ning into lampposts, we finally covered the seven blocks to the business section on White Plains Road. After banging into nine hundred baby carriages, asking count-less questions, and receiving much help, we made our way to the dime store. We wandered about. Finally, one of the counter girls took charge of us.

"What would you like to buy, boys?" she asked.

"Oh, nothing," I replied, "we're just shopping around."

For a moment she was confused, but, catching the smiles on our faces, she laughed. What a wonderful sound!

Her laugh meant that she thought of me as a person who couldn't see, and not as a blind person. When the adjective comes first, it sets the fence around the noun that follows. To be thought of as a person first, and then as not being able to see—this was the difference. From that moment I loved her. Her laugh was the real gate through which I passed, of which the other had been only the steel shadow.

Though Saturday-night dinner was known to us week-enders as "The Saturday Review"—consisting as it did of the week's leftovers—we enjoyed it. It was like a gathering of the Knights of the Round Table who met not merely to eat but to recount the day's adventures with our dragon—the subway. They were perilous, romantic, and funny. Compared with them, the bears, buffaloes, and avalanches of a Lewis and Clark did not seem very dangerous. After all, they could see them. For them, there were no open manholes that could swallow up a comrade without warning, no cart horses standing silently by a crosswalk, no automobiles turning right on a red light. On Saturday nights, when we left the leftovers again, we told tales of high adventure.

One Saturday night I was sitting next to Nick, a slow, fat, good-natured boy with a weakness for chocolate sodas that he indulged whenever he had fifteen cents, which wasn't often. After listening to a couple of narrow escapes from "the iron monster"—the subway—Nick began to chuckle softly to himself.

"What's the matter, Nick?" I asked.

"Well, a funny one happened to me today," he began, and instantly he had the floor. "I went down to the drugstore on Lydig Avenue to have a soda, see. I had my soda —a chocolate one—and I was coming out again when I knocked over some little kid. He began to yell like mad, so I picked him up and tried to stand him up, but he just fell over and kept on yelling. Well, I picked him up again, but he just kept yelling. Then some woman grabs me and starts shouting at me. 'What's the matter with you?' she yells. 'What are you trying to do to that little kid? How would you like it if someone tried to stand you on your head?' " Everyone roared as if we believed the story. Then someone chimed in, "Christ, you're as bad as that poor old blind man who was trying to sell brooms downtown last week. He was standing by the curb giving his spiel. Someone yanked a broom, so he says, 'Very good brooms, Mister. Fine brooms. Highest quality straw. Made 'em myself.' Someone yanked another one. 'There, that's a good one; they're all good. I can tell you. Would you like that one?' He finally got pretty sick and tired because the guy never said a word— just kept yanking at the brooms. He found out it wasn't anybody trying to buy the damn things. It was a horse standing there in the street eating them up."

"Yeah, that's pretty good," someone else said. "Reminds me of one I heard the other day. These two blinks were selling newspapers. This one guy had been selling on this corner for a long time, and along comes another blink horning in on his spot. They got arguing about who the corner really belonged to, and they got so mad they decided to have a fight right there. They put down their papers, and this one guy takes a mighty swing at the other. He missed and hit a horse standing by the curb. The horse hauls off and gives him a mighty kick and knocks him on his ass. After a minute he gets up, brushes himself off, and says, 'Jeez, I don't mind fighting, but goddamn, it ain't fair to throw rocks!' "

The Saturday Review was always full of hilarity. Humor was for us an avenue through which we momentarily escaped the sense of our own weakness, awkwardness, and vulnerability. In the moment of laughter, we pretended that we could see. Anyone fool enough to walk smack into a brick pillar deserved a knot on the head.

"What's the matter with you?" we would say, half choking a laugh. "You blind or something?"

That sort of thing could not possibly happen to us. It could not because we were pretending we could see. When some boy with a little vision laughed a little too often or a little too hard, we usually beat him up a little just for fun, and somehow that seemed to even things out.

But for us younger boys it was also a kind of class, for we had to study New York and its subways and elevateds more carefully than we ever studied geography. Our lives depended on our knowledge of the habits of the iron monster that coiled around and through the city. We made the older boys recite all the stops on the Seventh Avenue line from one end to the other while we memorized them. Then we made our own expeditions.

We learned on which side the doors opened at each stop, where the curves in the track were, and at what stations we would hear a bell and what it meant.

Sometimes we made mistakes. Fortunately, they were usually unimportant, such as getting off at the wrong station to make connection with another line. But sometimes they were more serious. Some fellows, for example, either did not know how, or were simply careless about stepping off the Seventh Avenue at 177 Street. In some places there was a gap of ten or twelve inches between the train and the platform, and ignorance or carelessness frequently resulted in a bruised shin or a twisted ankle as the monster nibbled at the leg in starting. Sometimes, though, accidents were the result of just plain bad luck.

One of my friends went to and from the Institute regularly by subway, and this involved changing from an Express to a Local at Forty-second Street. Forty-second, like many other downtown stops, is an island platform with trains running on either side, and this presents the most terrifying hazards to a person who is blind. The sounds of footsteps cannot be followed because one doesn't know how near the edge they are. Besides, the many echoes created by the walls, ceiling, and pillars of an underground station make it impossible to judge the distance and direction of sound. And where is the electric chasm of the other line? In changing from the Express to the Local, my friend had to cross such an island platform.

One day he stepped from the Express to hear the doors of the Local on the other side beginning to close. Habit had made him bold. He dashed across, stepped off the platform, and fell the five feet to the tracks. He was not on the train; he was in front of it.

As he hit the tracks the wheels began to move. Instantly realizing his danger, and with the speed and coordination he had developed on the mats—for he was an agile and powerful wrestler—he threw himself back against the wall. The beast ground past with every wheel brushing the lapels of his jacket.

After the rear end had gone by, he screwed up his courage to step back out on the tracks so he could get a grip on the edge of the platform. A passer-by saw him and gave him a hand. Once back on safe ground, he stood quietly collecting himself—then took the next train. The following morning he came to school in the usual way. He had been thrown by a horse, but he had to get back on, or capitulate. All of us had accidents, but we made light of them. We had to.

Sam seemed to be picked for bad luck. He pitched down open cellarways, got shaken up by cars, fell downstairs and off subway platforms. One day he fell off a platform, climbed back up, and stamped his feet furiously while hissing "shoo, goddamn you" to the goddess of misfortune, as if he were driving away a black cat or a witch.

Sam and I shared a passion for pizzas. When we could scrape up the cash on a week end, we would march off together in search of a pizzeria. When we had carfare, too, we would take the subway down to the lower East Side to look for new places. Finding a pizzeria in New York City is no easy job when you can't read. We depended on our noses. With a quarter in his pocket and a hunger pang in his stomach, Sam was like the Hound of the Baskervilles, relentless and sure. We trudged along, carefully sampling exhaust fumes until we finally hit the scent, and then there was no holding Sam. Occasionally we missed the right door and found ourselves looking for a table and asking for a twenty-five-center with cheese and tomatoes in the Chinese laundry next door, but these mistakes never dampened our enthusiasm.

However, it was really annoying to find our way into a bar whose doorway exhaled the unmistakable perfume of pizza, only to be taken by the bartender for a couple of drunks—and minors to boot—and to be kicked out even before we were properly in.

"All right, now," would come the gruff voice from behind the bar. "Go on, get back to where you got the rest of it."

"No! You don't understand. We just . . ."

"Out!" and heavy footsteps would thud around the end of the bar. At this point we usually left, but one day Sam was especially hungry and decided to stand his ground. Two big hands reached under his arms from behind, picked him up, carried him to the door, and set him down none too gently outside. In mock rage mixed with laughter, Sam turned, leaned inside the door, and shouted, "We just came here for a pizza. We're not drunk! What the hell's the matter with you? Are you blind or something?" The heavy footsteps pounded toward the door and we beat a hasty retreat.

One Sunday evening Sam and I visited our favorite pizzeria near the school. We walked in and began searching for a table. A blind person can do many things a person with sight can do, but looking for an empty table in a restaurant isn't one of them. Even when there are two of you, you just bump into twice as many tables and twice as many people.

This evening the place seemed to be full, and Sam and I had knocked into seven or eight chairs apiece when we gave up. Angry and ashamed, we stood still and waited to be rescued. Suddenly a hand grasped mine and dropped a quarter into it.

"No, no!" I cried. "We just want a table." But the hand was gone. Then the waiter recognized us.

"Hi, boys; over here. Cheese and tomatoes, eh?"

"Yeah," Sam growled.

As we sat there waiting, the quarter burned my palm. After a while I said, "Hey, Sam, some son-of-a-bitch gave me a quarter."

"What!" he cried incredulously. "Why, the dumb bastard!" and then the laugh broke through. "Damn it, Russell, I told you to dress up decent when you go out with me." The waiter slammed the pizza down between us. "Hey, waiter," Sam called, "give us another one with fish. My friend here is buying. Jeez, Russell, I knew you had to be good for something. When we finish these, I'll send you out to collect some more and we'll have a real feast."

When we got back that night, Sam told the story in a halfhearted way. He didn't go easy out of concern for my feelings; it was just that he knew the story wasn't worth much. It was too common. We were constantly being mistaken for beggars. You had to either cry or laugh, and, since you couldn't cry, you laughed, but not too hard.

7. That Other World

The Institute was our island sanctuary. Here we could work and play together in safety. The fence that confined us also protected us, and many of us grew to need the sweet poison of security. We were H. G. Wells' "Country of the Blind" come to life.

But I lived for three months each year outside the sanctuary, and it was not hard to tell the difference between these two worlds. In which was I to pass my life? This was the terrible question that weighed down my heart as I grew up.

I wanted to live outside, but could I? My knowledge of the other country came only from my vacations, but I knew my salvation lay there.

What were vacations like—those parallel bars that striped my life and to which I clung with the strong hands of memory during the long nights in New York as I lay in my room listening to the distant thunder of the elevated trains?

For four years my summers were long empty corridors down which I wandered, whiling away the hours in games of my own invention. I had my own private kind of baseball, played with a ping-pong ball and a small bat on a long stair landing. It was easiest there—it was almost impossible for the ball to escape me because of the banisters. I was player, umpire, and spectator all in one. I presided over this tiny world like God himself, and everything I wanted to happen did happen because I made it happen.

There were other amusements, too, such as the radio. I knew every serial on the air. "John's Other Wife" may have kept secrets from John, but I knew them all. I struggled down "The Road of Life" with Dr. Jim Brent. I hung on each sigh as "Joyce Jordan—Girl Interne" performed her tremendous feats of surgery. I sat crouched before the speaker entranced by Helen Trent's proving that "Romance can come to a girl when she is thirty-five or over."

When my father came home in the evening he would play tiddlywinks with me. Three games, a nickel a game. After I had won the three, which I regularly did, Hunnie and Mary and I went down to the corner for an ice-cream cone. If my father was too tired to play, he just gave me the fifteen cents and dispensed with the formalities.

Often after supper, when my father had settled himself on the front porch with his cigar and newspaper and my mother and Hunnie were doing the dishes, I would say in a casual voice, "This would be a good night to go to the Mangans, don't you think, Dad?"

"Well, you'd better ask your mother and see what she says."

I would rush to the kitchen and repeat my observation about this being a good time to see the Mangans.

"You'd better talk to your father," my mother would say. After having had seven children, neither of them would pass on any question before each knew the other's position. My mother and father would talk it over for a minute, and then we would go.

The Mangans were a large family with a big house about eight miles from Binghamton where they spent their summers. Peggy, the youngest, was Hunnie's age, and they were inseparable. Joe was six years older than I. His boundless enthusiasm and good nature made him one of my heroes. He never seemed to mind climbing trees with me and taking me on long explorations of the nearby hill.

As soon as my parents had agreed to go, Hunnie and I would run out to the barn and jump into the Packard where we waited for the grownups.

When they came, off we went down Front Street and out into the cricket-cool evening with the air full of the smell of hay. I opened the car window, leaned out, and took in the country. The fragrant hayfields were almost intoxicating, but no more vibrant than the rich brown smell of a newly manured garden. Then . . . did I catch the scent . . . was it . . . ? Yes, it was unmistakable now—somewhere ahead was a skunk. The scent grew stronger and stronger until, for a moment, it burned my nostrils, and then began to fade.

Soon we swung off the highway onto the old dirt road, crossed the little bridge over the creek, and then, at last, turned into the front yard by the big butternut tree. The old house lay back from the road behind a half acre of lawn. It was not magnificent, but it suited the Mangans themselves—big, open, and friendly.

It was a perfect place for children's games, and there were always plenty of kids to play them. It was marvelous for hide-and-seek—the places to hide were innumerable. We always played at night. Crouching in the bushes, the waxy buzz of grasshoppers and the chorus of small, shining cricket voices all about me, the hunted and the hunters suddenly thudded past through the wet grass. I knew I was being stalked down slowly and methodically by someone. Where was he? I could not tell, but wasn't that the sound of stealthy treads up in the garden? If it was, it would probably be Joe, who was "it." But it might not be Joe after all; and if it wasn't Joe looking for the rest of us, who was it?

The others were already snug in their hiding places and would not be creeping through the garden with such caution. Someone it was, coming so quietly toward me. Someone. Or perhaps it was not some*one*. It might be an animal come down from the hill, or, even worse, some *Thing* from another world stealing down upon a boy who thought he was hiding from other children, but who could not hide from this *Thing*. No! It was not in the garden. It was behind me—over by the barn. Or perhaps there were *two* ghosts! Not two, but *three,* for there was certainly something creeping along by the tennis court. The whole night was pregnant with things hunting me down.

Such were the shivering joys of summer nights at the Mangans. Summers meant the Mangans.

But there were Christmases, too. I would come home with my brother Jack, on his way from the University of Pennsylvania, or with Jimmy, coming back from Georgia Tech.

When we got off the train, the air was cold and sharp. Our feet crunched on the snow as we walked down the platform to where Mother and Dad waited with the car.

Binghamton had a curious smell, and getting off the train I always remembered with a sudden shock that what I had been missing was the smell of smoke and exhaust fume—odors as distinctive as the sound of my mother's voice. They meant home.

Christmas meant ice-skating, too. My sister Mary, who was five years older than I, used to trudge off with me to the park where we skimmed around and around the flooded and frozen football field.

There was also a toboggan slide. We set our toboggan carefully at the top, climbed on, wrapping our legs around the person in front, and then someone gave a little push. The snow hissed underneath the smooth wood, growing louder and louder, until with a scream of "Hang on!" we shot like a rolling thunderclap down the immense chute. *Bump!* We hit the ground and went sailing far out onto the broad field with a cloud of snow about us and the wind whistling in our ears.

Those were thrilling times, and Mary seemed tireless. She took me everywhere with her, and while she was not skating or tobogganing with me she was reading to me—anything and everything. She read very rapidly and had a throat of iron, for we often dashed through a dime novel about Doc Savage in an afternoon.

Our tree stands tall and brilliant in those vacations. Though I know my memory of how the tree looked must date from earlier days, its soft glow suffused those times for me. The very word "Christmas" glows crimson and green in the pine-sweet silence; the whisper of tissue paper under golden bars of ribbon. And always and ever is the sense of the white mystery outside the house that makes everything inside more secret, more fragile.

Early Christmas morning, at a signal from Hunnie, I crept from my bed and together we stole down the creaking front stairs. And then the tree! Hunnie passed me my presents. Almost always there was some kind of target set, either a bow with bristle-tipped arrows that would stick in the brush shield, or a gun that shot sticks with suction cups so they hit with a whang and stuck to a tin disk. One Christmas morning I found a bow and arrow set. I strung the bow and sent my first arrow crashing through the bulb of a big floor lamp, which was to be a present for my mother. I was faint with fear at the reprisals I expected to come at breakfast, but they never came. There was only an: "Oh, well, lucky it wasn't the window," from my mother.

On Christmas Day the scent of pine needles mingled

with the rich perfume of my father's cigar and, as the morning wore on, from the kitchen crept the warm, succulent smell of the turkey, dressing, and mince pies. Gradually it filled the whole house, and the last hour before dinner was hard to bear. And then we gathered round the long table for the family feast—first Mother; on her right Larry, Bud, and Jack; Jimmy at the corner; then Dad at the head; and on his right Mary, Hunnie, and me. I shall always cherish those early Christmases.

But even here, amid the chink and clatter of the holiday dinner, I was still in isolation. Though I was in that other world, I was not of it. My family and their friends accepted me completely, of course, but I had no real friends my own age. I must have understood something of my loneliness because, when I did make my first friend, I was overwhelmed with joy.

8. Steve

When I was ten I came home in June from my fourth year at the Institute just in time to be invited to Hunnie's class picnic at the State Park. My mother took us up to the park where the children had gathered, but they were too afraid of a blind child to play with me, or else they simply did not know how. After swimming all afternoon, we returned from the lake to the picnic tables.

I was a prodigious eater, and I outdid myself on that occasion. I devoured an impressive collection of hot dogs, a mountain of potato salad, and then settled down seriously to the business of demolishing a complete chocolate cake.

Eating is a fine art that growing children understand

and they are too naïve to deny their praise to anyone who excels in it. By the time I had started on the chocolate cake, my prowess had already attracted a circle of admirers who, by their explosions of delight and encouragement, made it clear they knew themselves to be in the presence of greatness. When I squeezed down the last mouthful there were cries of general acclaim, and the loudest of the voices was that of Steve Belansky, a boy who came from a home where they knew how to eat and valued a good appetite.

Three days later Steve came down to our house to pay his respects to the hero. By that time I had recovered from the indisposition that followed hard upon my display of gluttony, which had been so severe as to all but put me out of action on the day following the picnic. I was sorry not that I had eaten so much, but that I did not have a stronger constitution. My faith in my own capacity had been shaken, but Steve's appearance shortly afterward soon revived my spirits.

Steve and I became boon companions almost instantly, and we spent that and many more summers tramping along the Chenango River, fishing, swimming, and exploring. Steve had none of the usual attitudes toward blindness. He accepted it and immediately forgot it. He made no allowances. He expected me to be able to run just as fast as he did when a farmer caught us hooking a few ears of sweet corn to roast on the river bank for our lunch. He assumed I could climb any tree or fence he could climb, and so I did.

The following spring, Bud, my second eldest brother, married a charming nurse, and they lived in a little farmhouse about six miles from town. Steve and I would walk out there and spend the days just wandering about the countryside, using the farm for a base. Occasionally we did small jobs to justify our intrusion.

One day Bud commissioned us to chop down a little pear tree behind the house. We took turns hacking away inexpertly with a Boy Scout hatchet, and finally got almost halfway through the trunk. Then we tried to break it off, but there was too much spring in the tree.

"I've got an idea," said Steve excitedly. "Why don't you climb up into the tree, Bob? That'll give it more weight, and then it's sure to come down!"

I scrambled into the branches and swayed as hard as I could while Steve pounded away with the hatchet. *Snap! Crack! Boom!* Down came the tree. I lost my grip, rolled out of the branches and down a little bank. Not until I picked myself up and heard Steve's convulsions of laughter did I realize I had been tricked. My shame at the ridiculous position in which my trusting heart had placed me filled me with anger. Climbing into the branches of a tree so it could be chopped down! How could anyone be so stupid? And Steve . . . playing such a trick on a blind boy!

Ah! But there it was. He didn't care about my not being able to see. He would play a trick on me just as quickly as he would play one on anybody. That wasn't so bad; it was all right, really. No, it was pretty good. No! It was wonderful! Gee! It was the nicest thing anyone had ever done for me.

Off to the creek, then, at the foot of the hill for a whole lovely afternoon. The smallest bullhead or shiner was enough. We even had the courage sometimes to bring our catches back in our pockets. If Bud had been home long enough to settle down comfortably on the porch, he pretended to be amazed, and how I gloried in his wonder!

Our fishing rods were a permanent part of our gear whenever we turned down Front Street toward the outskirts of town, and our slingshots hung loosely from our shoulders. Slingshot. That key to joy—a powerful weapon capable of sending a small stone two hundred yards or more.

Steve introduced me to this weapon—a sturdy, nicely balanced crotch from an apple tree, two long strips of rubber carefully cut from an old inner tube, and a two-inch strip of soft leather. Of these essentials, the leather was the most difficult to come by. Once initiated, I searched for the leather with the enthusiasm of a dedicated amateur. I even cut the tongues out of a pair of my best shoes.

What did we do with our slingshots? No one who has ever been a boy could expect a complete and truthful answer to that question. On the whole, though, I didn't break as many windows as perhaps most boys take credit for. For one reason, windows were too easy to hit, and, for an even better reason, I didn't have much of a chance. Whenever we shot at a stationary target, Steve had to hit it first so I could place it, and, as every boy knows, windows aren't the sort of thing to stand up under more than one direct hit.

My forte was a moving target, anything that made a

noise when it moved. Most of our activity was confined
to the old city dump and the river bank where the rub-
bish attracted armies of vermin. Our pockets loaded with
stones, we declared open war upon the rat kingdom.

With long summer days of practice under Steve's careful instruction, I became a dead shot. Often I killed
rats invisible to him because their color blended in to the
background of rocks and ashes. Occasionally we were attacked by a rat, infuriated by a near miss or a shot that
had not finished him. We fled. These counterattacks lent
an element of spice and danger to the game—an angry
river rat is not a creature to be trifled with.

But the rats were never successful in pursuit. They
lacked the stamina and determination of the angry railroad workers at whom we sent our whistling missiles.
They responded manfully to the challenge. We always
had a good head start and always needed it. I developed
an extraordinary agility in clambering over fences, as
well as considerable speed.

These were skills that stood me in good stead in later
years and once, probably, saved my life. The railroad
workers never caught us, and perhaps that's why I still
feel guilty about having plagued them so shamefully.

One part of these mad flights always frightened me.
More than once we leaped to the top of a fence and onto
a garage roof. There was no time to let oneself down
carefully on the other side and then drop to the ground.
We had to jump, and jump without much preparation.
For me these were jumps into a bottomless pit.

I also had a BB gun. Naturally, this was secret. Because it was rather a large gun, it was difficult to hide. We usually kept it in the attic at 13 Edward Street, where we amused ourselves with target practice.

The third floor was a huge playroom. In its center stood a full-sized pool table with a rack of cues hanging on the wall. The table, shabby and with its cover sadly torn, now stood forlorn and unused, nothing more than a convenient place to heap all the odds and ends that collect in the attic of an old house. Here was the ideal hiding place for my gun, and I thrust it deep under a huge pile of old pillows and quilts I was sure would never be moved.

On rainy afternoons Steve and I would climb the stairs, first explaining to my mother that we were "just going up to play." She almost never went to the attic, so we could be certain of being safe there. Digging around one day, we discovered a big tin target dating from several Christmases before. It was ideal. We set it against one wall and, standing at the other end of the room, we had our shooting gallery. When it came my turn with the gun, Steve took one of the pool cues and tapped the tin target, whereupon I blasted away. At length I got pretty expert, so to keep things interesting we went on to more difficult shots.

My grandmother, when she was a little girl, had been given an expensive set of lovely doll's dishes. Children must have taken better care of their toys in those days, because the dishes came to my mother and then to my sisters intact, complete even with delicate sugar and creamer. I discovered this treasure carefully packed away in a big cardboard carton in a dusty corner, and my imagination immediately took fire. Here would be a real test of marksmanship.

Carefully placing a tiny cup on the rim of the target, we stepped back the twenty paces to the other wall and let fly. After twenty or thirty misses there was a crack!— and the fragments of the rare old hand-painted doll's cup tinkled to the floor. Huzza! The shot was not impossible, then. Exhilarated by the feat, we took another cup. It was my turn now. Steve put the cup in place and gently tapped the target directly beneath it. I popped away until the attic rang again with the tiny chimes of shattering china. This was real shooting.

That afternoon and many subsequent ones slipped peacefully by in this harmless pastime. The same imaginative genius that conceived the amusement also pointed out the hiding place for the telltale remains. There was a loose floor board under the cue rack, and it was a simple matter to sweep the pieces into the recess beneath it.

One day when the sport was at its height the door at the foot of the attic stairs quietly swung open and the steps of my mother approached. I ran to the pool table and fortunately had time to shove the gun under the pillows. Steve snatched up his broom to sweep away the evidence, but it was too late. We were caught red-handed. The floor was strewn with broken china, and we two boys stood with sheepish grins awaiting the inevitable. My mother could not appreciate my skill; she saw only the barbarous side of the affair. The enormity of my crime was brought home to me again and again, and yet again during the weeks that followed. The only remaining glimmer of joy in those dark days was the consolation that nobody knew about the gun.

My mother often took us to the river for a day's fishing. Before setting out, we smuggled the gun from the attic into the car, where we jammed it behind the cushion of the back seat. At the river one of us would distract my mother's attention long enough so the other could slip the gun out and shove it down a pants leg. Then off we would go for a day in heaven, wandering along the river bank, taking pot shots with the BB gun, and being, for hours without end, at one with the river and with each other.

9. Boyhood's End

To have Steve for a friend was to be rich, but my coffers overflowed when I found George. George Almstead and his parents worked a little farm right next to the Mangans' summer home. When we met he was fourteen and I was twelve. He was as devoted to fishing as I was.

As our friendship grew, I began to spend the nights with the Mangans and the days with George. George had Steve's disregard for my blindness.

One afternoon, sitting beside a little creek running through the pasture of a neighboring farmer, we were too deeply engrossed in our own thoughts to take much notice of the shiners nibbling at our bait and the cattle grazing about us. Gradually I became vaguely aware of a disturbance among the cows.

There seemed to be a lot of bellowing, but George was apparently unconcerned, so I ignored it. But ignoring the noise did not do away with it. It grew louder and louder and seemed to be coming closer all the time. I began to feel some anxiety when an animal lumbered into the alders behind us, snorting, snuffling, and giving short frequent roars that sounded like a locomotive approaching a crossing. I was not an expert in the calls of cattle, but this one sounded to me as if he were angry.

"George," I said, "doesn't it sound to you as though he's mad about something?"

"He!" said George skeptically, turning around. Instantly he sprang to his feet, shouting, "It's a 'he' all right—a big Holstein bull, and he's madder'n hell, and it's us he's mad at. Come on, here he comes."

As the enraged beast caught sight of us, he crashed after us through the thin screen of bushes. We flung our rods into the creek and dashed across to the other side. The water was not deep, but the mud on the bottom sucked off my loose-fitting moccasins at the first step.

"He won't come across," said George shakily. "Whoops! here he comes!"

And we dashed back across the stream with the bull close at our heels. George gripped my arm with one hand as we ran for our lives. He thought we couldn't make the distant fence, so he headed for the nearest tree about seventy-five yards away. The close-cropped grass of the pasture cut into my bare feet like a thousand tiny spears, but I didn't even notice it.

The moment we reached the tree was desperate. There were no branches for the first ten feet or so; and though I thought I could shinny up the tree, I didn't know whether I could do it in time, for the bull was hurtling down upon us.

"Okay!" said George breathlessly, "here we are. Up you go."

"No!" I cried. "You go ahead." Realizing this was no time for gallant banter, George fairly leaped up the trunk. I, in turn, had never climbed a flight of stairs more easily than I scrambled up that tree.

As we hung there in the branches, still shaking, the bull raged beneath us pawing the ground and digging his long horns into the earth, which he flung high into the air. He whetted his horns on the tree trunk and pounded it with powerful blows until the branches rocked and swayed.

"Do you think, George . . ." I stammered, "can a bull knock down a little tree like this?"

"No!" he said with forced assurance, "of course not. Well, I don't think he can. Whoops! I hope he can't," and the eight-inch trunk seemed to us at that moment as slender as a toothpick.

We shouted at the bull, trying to frighten him away, but we were the only ones who were frightened that afternoon. We shouted ourselves hoarse, but we never heard an answer.

After three hours, George saw the farmer coming down to take the cows to the barn. He heard our shouts for help, but when he understood our plight, to our dismay he retreated in haste.

"He's probably gone for help," said George, and it was true.

Twenty minutes later, four men armed with pitchforks fanned out from the pasture gate. One of them came up behind the bull and tried to attract his attention while another stole up toward the tree through some bushes to help us down. Suddenly the bull turned and made a wild charge at the farmer behind him. The other man leaped from the bushes to help us out of the tree, but we needed no assistance. We scrambled to the lowest branch and dropped to the earth.

But the bull apparently heard us and decided that, after all, it was those two boys he really wanted to grind into peopleburger, so he turned and thundered after us. We fled for our lives. George was the last to roll under the fence, with the bull only a few feet behind him.

The newspapers got hold of the incident, and next day carried a big headline: BLIND BOY FOILS BULL. They emphasized what they thought was the human-interest angle. They were wrong. They didn't understand at all. It wasn't a "blind boy" and a "sighted boy" up in that tree; it wasn't any white crow and black crow; it was just two boys—two friends—just me and George.

George's father, too, was a fisherman, and in the second year of our friendship, after two or three abortive tries, he finally got some neighbors to take care of the livestock so the Almsteads and I could spend a glorious week camping and fishing on the St. Lawrence River.

We found a place not far from Alexandria Bay where someone had started to build a few cottages; but they had laid only the floors. We nailed up canvas as a wind-break between us and the river and then collected hay and made deliciously comfortable and fragrant beds for ourselves. After knocking a hole in the bottom of a bucket and turning it upside down over a blowtorch, we had a stove on which Mrs. Almstead cooked some of the best meals I have ever eaten.

The St. Lawrence is a big river. That first night, lying on my bed of fresh hay, I heard the north wind booming in our canvas down out of Canada. The wind was big and soft, powerful and clean, like the river itself. Forty feet from our camp, the St. Lawrence rolled and slapped at the granite boulders lining the shore of our little cove.

The next morning Mr. Almstead drove into Alexandria Bay where he rented a flat-bottomed boat. Hooking on the outboard motor, he came chugging back to camp. George and I with all our gear jumped in almost before he touched shore, and we swung out into the river for a day of warm sunshine, river smells, and the sound of fish lapping on the boards. They were just lowly sunfish, rock bass, and bluegills, but even they are big on the St. Lawrence. Everything is big up there. These fish were of the same family as the little potlickers and bait snatchers that infest the waters downstate, but they weighed anywhere from half a pound to a pound and a half.

George and I caught none of the big northern or wall-eyed pike, black bass, or muskelunge for which the St. Lawrence is famous, but then, we never seemed to catch big fish anywhere. We attributed our lack of success to the fact that there was blasting over on the Canadian side—we could hear the dull thunder of the explosions. But if it hadn't been the blasting, it would have been the wind, or the temperature, or the air pressure, or any of a thousand things.

Despite the blasting, there were people catching a few big ones, and some of them were camped right next to us, the Havens from Cortland. We used to collect around the Havens' campfire at night because Mr. Haven had a chart of the St. Lawrence and he fished that river as it ought to be fished. Mr. Almstead and George took a real interest in the chart, but I had another interest.

There on the banks of the great St. Lawrence I fell in love. Her name was Adele Haven; its chime still has silver magic. She was twenty and I was thirteen. She said she liked acorns, so I plunged through the undergrowth that quivered with mosquitoes in search of them.

"I'm going to paint them different colors," she said, "and sew them onto my moccasins as a kind of fringe. See,"—and her soft hand took mine—"I've half finished this one."

My fingers tingled as she ran my hand over the soft leather of her shoe—a woman's shoe. "You brought me these yesterday. This one is red, this is green, and this is yellow. They are going to be very gay when we've finished."

She cared enough to explain and show me, and that made all the difference.

Though first love is ridiculed by those who can no longer remember it, it was not ridiculous to me. Probably more than other children, I had been profoundly self-centered. In loving Adele, I took the first step from the shore of my boyhood. Had she been other than what she was, that week on the St. Lawrence could have been a disastrous turning point in the life of a boy painfully conscious of his oddity. Her kindness and gentleness led me to hope that I might someday be loved by a girl from the other world, a girl who could see.

10. Memory and Desire

It was to that world—the bull, the BB gun, the sling-shot, and the St. Lawrence—that I clung in my iron bed at the Institute during the long nights in New York.

Then I would slip back to the banks of the Chenango and fish and gossip and remember with George and Steve. I felt again the cool, silent depths of the river beneath my boat, smelled the damp, dark smells about me, and heard the hiss of my fly rod and line and the tiny splash of the bait. The redwings whistled in the soft whisper of branches along the shore. The slap, slap of the water against the bow, and the soft, cool rushing sound of the riffs upstream grew and subsided as the summer breeze rose and fell.

Here, alone on the water, under a blue memory of sky with white puffballs in slow motion rolling and toppling about the universe, I found myself in a kind of suspended animation. The world, as it were, slowed down so that a boy whose senses were not as keen or quick as eyesight could look at it, could come to know what it was, and could discover where he fitted into it.

Summer had taught me the sounds, the smells, the taste and the feel of nature. I had learned what it was to plant my heart, mind, and soul in the mystery of earth and water. As the fish darts from darkness into sunshine, as the tree and the grass stretch up toward light, I, too, was beginning to push from my dark captivity toward freedom.

My hateful infirmity that bound me with chains stronger than steel to my schoolfellows tore at me as I struggled. I had the deep sense that this bond, however firm and terrible, was artificial. Most of my classmates seemed not to chafe in bondage. But I did.

When I was with Steve or George or alone on the river I could believe that I would fit in. I was *not* strange, and this memory gave me the strength to reject the sanctuary and to set out to join the world outside.

For years I had waged a campaign to escape from the security of the Institute as soon as possible. At the end of the sixth grade I took some of the State Regents examinations designed for eighth-graders, and passed. Then I took the rest after the seventh grade. Having skipped the eighth grade, I settled down to compressing four years of high school into three.

I had decided that I wanted to be an osteopath, and

I had thought I needed a B.A. degree first. Though I had four brothers, each one had gone to a different college, so we had no family loyalties to guide me. The Mangans were staunch supporters of Hamilton College in Clinton, New York, and Joe Mangan in particular had been filling me with tales about it. Unknown to my parents, I made out my application for Hamilton and shipped it off just before Christmas of my senior year. I had declared firmly that I needed a substantial scholarship, so it was quite a shock to my father when he received a letter from Hamilton College requesting a full statement of his financial position. He sent the statement, and I received a scholarship.

I knew that going to college would be the crucial test of my life. Was I crippled? Could I grow up by memory?

On a warm June day in 1941, ten years after the gates had clanged behind me for the first time, I walked through them for the last time. I said good-by to Bob Rossiter, Merritt Clark, Fred, Sam, and the rest. My feeling about the Institute did not soften the pain of leaving them, for no friendships are ever so intense again as those of one's school days.

As steel struck steel in the old familiar way, a period of my life was closed the significance of which I would not understand for years.

Two: THE ASCENT

11. Departure and Arrival

Early in August the Hamilton Alumni Association sponsored a picnic at the Mangan's country house for prospective freshmen. Small groups of nervous hopefuls listened attentively to the consciously sophisticated banter of their betters. We quivered with respect before the nonchalant upper classmen who were indoctrinating us.

"It's pretty rough up there," my hero was saying, "plenty rough. You're damn lucky. They don't take everybody, you know; and even then lots of them don't last."

Suddenly an authoritative voice demanded we all be quiet. "All right, it's time to get down to business, and I want to say a few things to you fellas who are interested in going to Hamilton—up to The Hill, as we call it. You may think college is just a lot of parties like this where everyone enjoys himself, but that's not true, is it, Kegs? Kegs is a senior like me, so he really knows what it's all about. It isn't just a lot of parties where everyone has fun, is it, Kegs?"

"Hell, no!" drawled a voice from a cloud of pipe smoke. "It's rugged."

"Hear what Kegs says? It's a serious business."

"That's right!" came from the foggy corner called Kegs.

"The thing about it is, you see," continued the chairman, "that you're not in the bush leagues any more when you're a Hamilton man. It's something to be proud of. All of us are proud we're men from The Hill, aren't we?"

"Damn right!" growled the fog bank.

"What I wanted to say is just this: It isn't all fun and games. It's hard to get into Hamilton and hard to stay there. That's why we love it and are proud of it, and we know you'll all love it, too."

This seemed to end the formal program, for the college men yawned, stretched themselves, and lounged out to the cold beer.

That evening I met two people who were to become fast friends, Ken Whiting and his younger brother, Ted. Ken was a junior and seemed amazingly unimpressed by his exalted status; and Ted, like myself, was a green aspirant. I think Ted probably spoke only eight words that night to people other than his brother, which was four or five more than I spoke to people other than Joe

Mangan. It was Joe's irrepressible good humor and Ken's quiet reassurance that kept firm my resolution to go up to The Hill.

Would I ever capture their poise, assurance, and nonchalance? For some time I had been surreptitiously practicing the art of pipe smoking and had made some progress, but it would be useless to pretend I could down a beer with anything like comfort, let alone pleasure. Since I planned to give up smoking to get in shape for the wrestling season that first semester, my predicament would be hopeless, for, with my pipe gone, the sole prop of my quivering ego would be taken from me.

The weeks slipped away and September crept upon me. Joe, who had graduated the previous June, had arranged for me to ride up with Bill, a friend of his who was returning for his last year. On a lovely Sunday afternoon we jammed my suitcase into the already overloaded trunk of Bill's car and I said good-by to my parents. How different was this good-by from all those others! Instead of the usual lump in my throat and the anger in my heart, I felt only a profound concern about my knees.

Soon we were sweeping along the broad highway in a car crowded with returning students. About halfway we broke the ninety-mile drive by stopping for a few beers. The others had the "few" while I struggled with my one. I made a vain attempt to take enough bottled courage to make the rest of the journey successful and happy, but the single beer inspired only a feeble show.

As we drew near Hamilton, the excitement of my companions increased while my spirits sagged. Suddenly the tires began to whir on the corrugated concrete pavement leading up the hill on top of which stood the college.

"You're in South Dorm, aren't you, Bob?" asked Bill.

"Yes," I replied, and my voice sounded like a stranger's. Soon the car ground to a stop on the gravel beside South Dorm. The door opened, suitcases bumped and grumbled in the trunk, and suddenly I was being helped out.

Habit prompted me to reach for the familiar gate, but, of course, there was no gate, no fence, nor, farther in the distance, the swirling city of New York. There would be no rigorous regimentation, no bells buzzing commands in the impersonal tones of authority. But, at the same time, neither would there be the old familiar concrete walks whose every turn I knew; no buildings through which I could move with as much assurance as through my own home; no athletic field in which to play the old games, and no Bob Rossiter and Merritt Clark with whom to share the old familiar complaints and resentments. As I mounted the four flights of stairs to my room, I was stepping up into a new life—a life both wonderful and terrifying!

Bill dropped the suitcase, opened the door, and said, "Here we are. Hello, fellows. This is your roommate, Bob Russell."

"Hello, I'm Doug Mitchell."

"Hi, I'm Frank Green. Come on in."

"Well, I'll see you later," Bill said. "You fellows show

him around, will you?" and he clattered off down the stairs.

We had one large room with two small bedrooms adjoining it. We flipped coins, and Doug and I ended up sharing one bedroom, leaving the other to Frank.

After I had unpacked, the three of us settled down with the college catalogue to see what sense we could make of it and to try to make out our schedules. We did this together because the schedule of each was important to the others. New York State contributed $300 per year to each blind resident attending an approved college. I had turned over the disbursement of this money to Hamilton, which, in turn, offered it as work grants to students who were willing to read. Doug and Frank had both accepted, so the college had made us roommates. Obviously it would be most sensible for us to take the same courses so that, while reading to me, they would also be doing their own assignments.

We were immersed in the all but impossible task of translating the language of the catalogue into understandable English when there was a knock at the door, and in walked Ken Whiting. With the skill of a virtuoso he riffled through the catalogue and gave us a brief and simple account of the various courses, together with sound advice. In twenty minutes most of our problems were solved and, as he rose to leave, he invited us all to dinner at the L. C. House, a fraternity of which he was president, at the foot of the hill.

That evening Doug and I tramped down to the house, where I suffered in silence through a long, for-

mal dinner. After the hum and buzz and clatter of the
meal, we adjourned to the sitting room, where the freshmen were pried loose from one another and entertained
by genial L.C.'s.

The fraternal conversation that had filled the sitting
room since dinnertime now began to sputter and cough.
Instead of one group, there now seemed to be several
small ones from which came an occasional guffaw. The
social organism was breaking down. Fellows were drift-
ing toward the door to creep upstairs either to a book
or to suitcases not yet unpacked. The chairman of the
Rushing Committee, sensing what was happening, made
a valiant effort to revive the flagging spirits of the
gathering by calling out, "Hey! Who's for a show in
Utica?"

A ripple of question and assent spread quickly through
the room, and freshmen rose to their feet in relief. Ken
Whiting came over, took me aside, and asked gingerly
if I went to movies.

"Yes, I do, but"—and I stretched for what I thought
might be the first rung on the ladder of success—"but
perhaps some of the other fellows might like to stop
somewhere for a beer." I was aghast at my own bravado,
but it was a lucky shot.

"Would you like a beer?" Ken almost whispered.
"Keep still, then, till the others have gone."

In a few minutes the sitting room was almost empty.
After ushering the last lot out and into a car, Ken returned and shouted up the stairs, "Anybody want to go
to Frank's?"

The upper stories came to life. Chairs were shoved

back, suitcases and trunks slammed shut, feet thudded on the stairs, and voices cried, "Just a second," "Be right there," "Hey, wait a minute, will you?" In a matter of moments seven L.C.'s and one frightened freshman were stacked into an ancient Ford, and a series of sharp explosions under the hood shattered the quiet of the evening. As we rolled out of the driveway, a pair of flying feet pounded across the gravel and a latecomer leaped onto the running board where he clung for the two-mile trip.

Frank's was like a boiler factory, and there were plenty of boilermakers at work. All Hamilton seemed to be there—all but the Rushing Committees who were soberly entertaining freshmen at movies. Ken seemed to know everyone, and he introduced me to all his friends. I must have bent elbows with a hundred Hamiltonians.

To my astonishment, in these surroundings and atmosphere the beer seemed to go down quite easily. By the third, it even began to taste good. By the fifth, I was shaking hands without embarrassment. I was the first blind student to be admitted to Hamilton since its founding, but these fellows didn't seem to care. My proposal to have a beer had been a success. Unwittingly I had put my right foot forward, and it rested comfortably with those of other Hamiltonians on the common ground of Frank's bar rail.

After thundering back to the fraternity house in the relic of Ford's early genius, we raided the refrigerator. Then someone suggested a bridge game. Instantly I produced a deck of Brailled playing cards that I had thoughtfully left in my jacket. It was an ordinary deck that I had marked in the corners with Braille. When the bidding was over, I asked to have the dummy read, and to have each card called as it was played. Thereafter, as with other card games, I operated by memory. No magician ever pulled a better rabbit out of his hat. We settled down on the living-room floor for two rubbers of bridge, and then the relic, with Ken Whiting at the wheel, coughed and complained its way up the hill to South Dorm.

The following morning Doug, Frank, and I went over to the chapel for the first official meeting of the class of '45. We sat quietly through the long speeches from college dignitaries. The sermonizing over, the Dean rose to tell us of the Freshman-Sophomore Day to be held that Saturday. It was to consist of an athletic competition, and, to my great joy, one of the events was to be wrestling. There were to be three bouts, a lightweight, middleweight, and heavyweight, and the Dean called for volunteers to represent us in these divisions.

With my heart in my mouth and supporting myself by hanging onto the back of the seat in front of me, I volunteered as the freshman heavyweight and sank back into my seat. My proposal was greeted with a stunned silence from my hundred and thirty classmates. As the silence thickened, I realized they were probably trying to think of how to reject my offer without publicly embarrassing me. I struggled to my feet again and said that of course I understood my offer was only a challenge to wrestle any other volunteers for the right to represent '45. The Dean finally broke the silence by saying that this was the way positions on a team were usually decided, and the meeting proceeded.

During the next five days I went through the regular "freshman orientation," but I recall only the afternoons I spent in the gym trying to limber up my stiff muscles for Saturday and also to be on the spot to meet anyone who wanted to challenge me for the heavyweight position. The days passed and no challengers appeared. By Saturday morning I felt certain I was to be the freshman heavyweight. I was light for a heavyweight, but I had hopes of making at least a reasonable showing.

The class of '45 won the first event and kept on winning. About fifteen minutes before the wrestling matches, I went back to the dorm with Doug to put on my sweat clothes. We returned just in time for the beginning of the first bout. The lightweights began to whirl and roll about on the grass before the crowd of spectators. Doug was trying to explain to me what was happening when he was interrupted by our temporary class president, a big football player, who tapped me on the shoulder and took me aside.

"Look, Bob," he said, "the sophomores have put up a huge tackle from last year's team. We all think it's great of you to have offered to wrestle for us, but it's not too late to change your mind. I've been working out this last week, and I'm all ready to go. What do you say?"

I realized no one had taken my offer seriously. They never really expected me to go through with it, and they had quietly selected a substitute in whom they had placed their confidence.

"No," I answered. "If you wanted to wrestle today, you should have challenged me yesterday or the day before. Since you didn't, you have no right to take my place." I was very nervous, as I always was before a match, but I knew that more was riding on this bout than on any I had ever wrestled before.

"Nobody will think badly of you," he continued; "don't be afraid of that."

But I didn't want them simply not to think badly of me. I wanted them to think well of me.

"No! I'm going to wrestle."

"Well, okay, then. Good luck."

My turn came at last, and I walked to the center of the clearing in the crowd. The referee asked for silence so that I could hear the footsteps of my adversary as we approached each other. He need not have asked because as I walked out a hush fell over the field.

As soon as we came together, I knew I would have my hands full: my opponent outweighed me by thirty-five pounds, none of which was fat. Not knowing what would really be cricket for him to do, he felt the awkwardness of his position. This uncertainty was his downfall, for I was merciless. I tripped him quickly and, as he fell, slipped a half nelson on and rolled him over onto his back. He struggled furiously when he understood what was happening, but it was too late. The crowd burst into cheers while the referee pounded the turf to signify a fall.

However, the rules called for two out of three falls, so the match was far from over. I knew that in the second bout he would have no qualms about my blindness and was probably furious at his public humiliation, so the minute's rest between bouts gave me much-needed time to consider how I should try to handle him.

"All right," cried the referee, "time's up," and we started again at each other across the grass. I proceeded warily toward the sound of his footsteps, but all my caution was useless. With a tremendous charge he sent me sprawling and was on me like a tiger. His strength and anger made him impossible to handle, so I let him shove me about without trying to match the fury of his attack. It would have been useless for me to try out-muscling him; I simply had to wait until he gave me an opening.

Finally it came. He reached an arm under mine in an attempt to turn me over. I clamped down on his arm above the elbow and put all my strength into a roll that carried me around, dragging him beneath me. I quickly turned, let go his arm, and I was on top. Immediately I put a scissors grip on him and flattened him. When he tried to get onto his hands and knees, I kicked his legs out from under him, at the same time knocking his arms forward. Again he found himself on his stomach.

After several futile attempts to get up, he started to roll furiously in the hope of doing to me what I had done to him. He was much too big and too powerful for me to stop these rolls; instead, I simply gave his roll added impetus so that in place of a half roll, which would have left him on top of me, we performed a complete turn so that he was still on the bottom. After he had tired himself out in these struggles, I put on a half nelson and turned him over, and pinned him again.

The crowd roared once more, and the referee raised my arm in victory. There seemed to be hundreds of people pounding me on the back, shaking my hands, and practically carrying me from the field of battle. That day, when the shoulders of the big tackle pressed against the grass for the second time, I began to win a place at Hamilton.

If I had passed up my chance to wrestle I might have passed up a college career and much more besides. It was a chance to make a definite, violent, and public declaration that I was not peculiar, not weak or afraid, and would not be ignored; that I neither expected nor would accept any concessions to my blindness.

I have known several blind college students. Some of them who were eminently well qualified to do the academic work gave up their hopes and quit; they could not stand the loneliness. In the midst of the turmoil and camaraderie—the football games, the dances, the beer parties, poker games, bull sessions, workouts at the gym—in the midst of all these they lived lives of seclusion and despair. How could they break in? How could they become part of this friendly ferment?

For me, the first night at Frank's bar and the big sophomore tackle were the doors by which I began to enter into the college community. Some, though, cannot find a door. Anything will do—a talent for music, a gift for telling dirty jokes. Anything so long as it is used. I used what I was lucky enough to possess and was saved from a loneliness that probably would have driven me back home.

My wrestling and beer drinking had defined me as a

certain kind of person—the Joe College sort. I had to preserve this reputation and, if possible, enlarge upon it, or at least fill in the details. For example, I drank, but how much could I drink? I'm sure this was of no interest to anyone but myself, and yet I wanted to make my capacity a matter of public knowledge. Memories of the chocolate cake victory seven years before inspired me to another feat of gluttony.

As publicly as I could, I declared I would drink a whole quart of wine the coming Sunday afternoon, and then I commissioned one of my friends to buy the wine —a sickish sweet Port.

I was disappointed that the event didn't draw a bigger crowd. However, unabashed, I tried to make up for the lack of spectators by enriching the ceremony. At the advertised hour, I undressed, got into my pajamas, and climbed into bed, which I had surrounded with pipes, ash trays, radio, typewriter—indeed, with all the things necessary for a long and impressive sojourn. I then carefully uncorked my bottle. By this time, though, only two or three fellows were hanging around, and they were clearly there because they wanted Doug Mitchell to help them with their English. I took a few lusty swigs, lit my pipe, turned on a Giants' football game, and began to type my English composition.

Swigging, typing, smoking, and listening, I got through the first hour, but then somebody made a touchdown, my pipe started to bite back, my typewriter got stuck, and the wine began working. It didn't suffuse me with its advertised sense of well-being. Instead, it sent out waves of increasing size and frequency from a central nausea. With a confused concern about the game, a burning tongue, fingers that twitched nervously on the keyboard, and a growing grievance at my middle, I began to lose interest in my public experiment. The real trouble was that it wasn't public at all. No one even cared.

My exhibition was a fiasco. It was no exhibition because there was no audience. I didn't have a show worth seeing. Why not, I wondered? This would certainly have gone over big at the Institute. If I had pulled it there, I would have gone down in history as one of the arch malefactors of all time. But at Hamilton the fellows on the same floor couldn't be bothered even to walk across the hall to get a free look. I wasn't a malefactor in their eyes; indeed, I wasn't even interesting. I must, I thought, certainly now be in that big, cold world I had heard so much about. But that was what I had wanted, wasn't it? I had better cut my losses and get on.

I got up, put the half-empty bottle in my bureau drawer, dressed, went over to the cafeteria for some coffee, and, somewhat bedraggled and at least a little wiser, returned to my room and settled down to writing a letter to a girl from Mercihurst College whom I had recently met.

To be at a men's college and not to have a girl, at least to talk about, would be as silly as setting out to sea in a colander. The bull sessions at Hamilton, after starting on Pope Gregory VII, Joe Louis, James Joyce, or Benny Goodman, always ended up on women. If you didn't have a particular girl to talk about—two or three were even better—you might as well go back to your

room and study history or go to bed. Penny was my
gambit. I could put the hardiest to sleep with a recital
of her virtues. I could even outdo Joe Ward, who had a
very strong thing in someone called Boots.

It became embarrassing, though, when I never could
produce Penny. All the other fellows brought their girls
to the Fall House Party, Winter Carnival, or Spring
House Party. I asked Penny to come to all three, but she
never came. Either she couldn't scrape up the money for
the train fare, or the connections between Erie and Utica
were no good, or she had broken her leg playing ping-
pong, or she had contracted ptomaine poisoning from a
can of sardines. Anyway, she never came. This made me
miserable, for I loved her as only a sixteen-year-old can
love. But what was much more serious, I needed her
desperately to preserve my shaky status in the woman
department among the fellows on the fourth floor.

Though she never accepted my invitations, she did
write me glorious letters saying how much she missed
me. Her letters had to be read to me, and I did my best
to pick a different reader each time. Thus Penny's exist-
ence, as well as her depth of feeling for me, were firmly
established.

I threw the weight of my genius into writing letters
and chose the moments for their composition with great
care. Indeed, I took more care about the choice of the
time than with the letters themselves.

I usually wrote on week ends, because then I could
count on a hot blackjack game being in progress in our
room. When the game became really tense, when two or
three had lost their next week's allowances and were

fighting to regain them, when the winners were taut with the thrill of wealth and the immediate prospect of more, at such moments I would push my chair back with, "Damn! Deal me out, will you, Frank? I forgot to write to Penny this week." I would go to my desk, pull out my portable, and begin hammering away furiously.

It was adolescent theater, but then, it was an adolescent audience. Once in a while someone else would follow my lead and pull out with the same excuse, but these seemed second-rate and distinctly hammy.

Though I never actually produced Penny for inspection, I did get a date for the first Fall House Party. Ken Whiting asked me to come to the party at the L. C. House. I turned up early Friday afternoon with my two bottles of whisky. Ken wrote my name on the labels and put them up behind the bar. Then we went into Utica to pick up my date at the station. It was very sweet of Janet to come, though I'm certain she did so more in the hope of meeting some attractive upperclassmen than for the pleasure of my company. She was a sophomore at a college in Albany, and I, a lowly freshman.

At these parties, the girls take over the fraternities for the week ends and the fellows move up to sleep in the dorms, so Jan was installed at the L. C. House, and Ken and a few other L.C.'s brought their things up to South Dorm.

There was an informal dinner Friday night, followed by dances at all the fraternities, a football game Saturday, a formal dinner at the fraternity that evening, and then a college dance in the gym. Jan put up with my shyness, awkwardness, and, even more noble of her, my moments of bravado.

I began the party Friday evening very ill at ease. What on earth did people talk about on dates that lasted three days? What could a young freshman say to a sophisticated sophomore?

Added to this was an acute realization of my clumsiness in the simple amenities of social life. For example, I didn't know when to pass Janet the ash tray; indeed, if I had known, I didn't know where the ash tray was. I didn't know when to offer her another drink. I couldn't tell her how nice she looked.

Whether Janet felt anything of this I don't know. But I felt it acutely, and it made me ashamed, ashamed because I was blind. If I was ashamed of myself, how despicable must I not be in the eyes of a girl who had the misfortune to be my date?

At this first house party, as on the first night of college, I turned to alcohol. This partially relaxed my tension and brought some relief. About midnight, Janet, seeing that I was already two sheets to the wind and recklessly unfurling the third, sensibly took herself off to bed.

As soon as she left, I began to enjoy myself, not because I was relieved to be rid of her, but because I no longer had the feeling of not being able to do for her the things I thought I should do. With no further sense of incompetence and shame, I was relaxed and confident, and had a glorious time.

The next morning Janet heard of my successes with

the other girls, my gaiety, geniality, and wit. She did not, I am sure, believe it. Once again I had to assume impossible responsibilities and, with the added misery of a hangover, I was stupidity itself.

But there were times when I avoided crowds. A hissing, clicking, snarling hockey rink is no place for anyone who can't see. Whenever I took to the ice at the regularly scheduled times, I had to go *with* someone and either hang on or be hung on to. This is like going for a swim while clinging to a rowboat.

So when the others were at lunch I used to go over to the rink, put on my skates, and push off into emptiness. I felt like an eagle, long caged, whose bars had been opened.

The encircling board fence was tall enough to echo the "sh-sh" of my steel, and I glided across the ice rejoicing in the release of power. Lampposts, curbs, baby carriages, and trees early teach a blind person the wisdom of caution, but he must always chafe under its restraint. To be on the open, empty rink was for me to be able to see, and I threw off my chains. I would whip down at top speed and, for the sheer joy of it, put off my turn till the last instant, when, sharply swinging off, I brushed the boards with my shoulder.

One day someone left the goalie's cage on the rink and I nearly drove it through into the swimming pool; thereafter I took a slow, exploratory turn before letting loose.

*

When two sighted people meet, each has the option of starting a conversation. A blind person does not have that option. If a hundred people with whom I would have liked to talk passed me without speaking, it would be for me as if they had not passed at all. Footsteps have no names. Until he is greeted, a blind person is a particle of the random element outside a whirring mechanism. The greeting is a line that pulls him back from the void and incorporates him.

All these things—beer-guzzling, dating, cardplaying, and wrestling—constituted in varying degrees my bid for recognition. They were the symbols of my belonging to this new world. People were beginning to say hello.

12. Becoming Spring

The summer of 1942 was different from all those other peaceful and sunny, but constricted, islands of earlier years. During my last year in high school I had studied massage in the evenings, so chafing and kneading the golfers at a nearby country club was a pleasant way of earning pocket money. Now I also had friends to spend it with. The Whitings lived in Binghamton and we used to go out together for a few beers in the evening. It was the normal thing to do. That is why it was special.

Those earlier summers had been so many retreats, retreats into the secret joys of the river. George and Steve and I had tramped the banks of the Chenango, snatched corn from nearby fields, and roasted it with our catch on the rocks. And there were times when, for whole days together, I rode anchor alone in a little boat, soaking in the sunshine and the rain, sending forth the tendrils of life to take root in the slapping of the water in the shallows, the rushing of the riffs, and the song of the redwings along the shore. This, or much of it, was beginning to pass.

The intensity of those days was starting to slacken, and that summer the pleasures of the river were being replaced. My base was broadening; I was breaking out of the protective shell of my secret life and starting to live in a world wide and free, one that held the promise of growth. The Whitings were my first close friends in this New World.

There had been Steve and George, but they were boyhood comrades, and there is a difference between boyhood companions and friends. George and Steve and I were all worshipers at the shrine of nature, consecrated to our slingshots and air rifles. We simply had the good luck to find one another at the same shrine. Each liked the way the other wore his weapons, so we took to praying together.

A mature friendship presupposes a basic respect for another's privacy. Among George, Steve, and me there was no such respect, because we were not conscious of grounds on which we would resent trespassers. The outdoors was our common mistress, and nature, like Chaucer's Duchess, could easily give a light to the lamp of an admirer without diminishing the store of her own fire.

I was going back to Hamilton in the fall without any

of the previous year's misgivings or uncertainties. I knew the campus, the classrooms, a few of the professors and most of the students, and, above all, the conventions of the place. Though I had sacrificed my studies, I did fit in socially, and I knew it.

At one of the fraternity beer parties toward the end of my first year I left the bar to visit the men's room. A friend followed me and snapped on the light—reasoning, I suppose, that since I couldn't see, I wouldn't be able to find the switch. Suddenly he realized how ridiculous he had been: "You son-of-a-bitch! Why didn't you stop me?"

And, snapping off the light, he retreated to the bar, laughing. The sudden hush at the bar, the droning of one voice, and then the gales of laughter proved he couldn't keep such a good joke to himself, even though it had been on him. Following to help out had been automatic courtesy, like passing the salt. He had not been "being kind." The fellows at the bar, too, had not felt themselves under any constraint because of my blindness. They laughed because it was funny, and when I came back, they asked me to take them to the men's room.

I had directed most of my energies in the first year toward proving to everyone on campus and to myself that I was quite normal and belonged. Now I no longer had to prove that point. The era of exhibitionism was over. I had become just another undergraduate in everyone's eyes, and, like the others, I turned my attention to books.

Our increased preoccupation with books was partially

the result of a desire to escape from thinking of the gulfs that had opened before us. We spent our time grappling with the present so as not to have leisure to look toward the future.

However, halfway through the second year, something happened that forced me to think about the future— indeed, changed my whole conception of time.

The telephone rang one evening after dinner. It was a call from Binghamton—my mother's voice saying, "I think you'd better come home, Rob. Dad's in the hospital. He's had a heart attack."

I took the next bus to Binghamton in a daze.

Of course, I knew everyone had to die, but I never believed "everyone" included my father. It had always been easy to accept mortality as an idea, but now it seemed that I might have to accept it as fact. My father, who twelve years before had walked up and down the hall outside my bedroom door in anguish, the man for whom it was the greatest misery to see another suffering —what was he now not suffering himself?

He had taught me how to play marbles, taken me to baseball games, to the races at Saratoga. On those special nights when a boxing match was broadcast, crouched before the radio we had feasted on crackers and cheese with a small glass of wine for me. He went back to the beginnings of everything. That he should stop being, that he should die—this was impossible.

When I arrived home, everyone was there. Jack, who was a Captain in the Air Force stationed at Mitchell Field, had just arrived; and Mary, who had been married the year before, had come home from Wilmington. Jimmy had come from Chattanooga, Tennessee, where he was making maps for the War Department.

None of us had ever been demonstrative, and even now no one dared show what he was feeling.

That night at the hospital my father seemed his old, cheerful self, but the doctor was not so sanguine. "It's impossible to tell with these coronaries," he explained in a whisper in the hall. "He might be all right for the next twenty years, but in his present condition the next attack will probably be the last. But he may not have another attack. There's just no telling."

Swift nurses flitted up and down the corridor where we stood in a tense knot breathing in the hygienic sterility of the hospital. Their impersonal cheerfulness intensified the aloneness of this drama. The waiting, the watching, the hope, and the fear belonged to us.

Only my mother was permitted to sit in the room with him. The rest of us went in singly for a few moments and then came out to rejoin the others.

One morning I woke to find myself sitting on the edge of the bed tying my shoes. Someone must have called me. There were footsteps and sobs in the hall. It was over, then.

The death of someone you love is something so huge that it takes time to grasp fully as a fact. Even when it is grasped, it is so overwhelming that it cannot be held for very long at one time. It comes and goes as the spirit struggles and fails to keep it on the perimeter of consciousness.

Thus for the three days of the formalities that follow

death, we rode out the storm of knowledge, now sub-
siding to half knowledge and then rising again to crests
of intensity.

> The Bustle in a House,
> The Morning after Death
> Is solemnest of industries
> Enacted upon Earth—
>
> The Sweeping up the Heart
> And putting Love away
> We shall not need to use again
> Until Eternity.

Eternity is such a big word. My father's death was
definite, irrevocable, provisional upon nothing. He would
never come home again.

This year had been for me my introduction to life, as
it were, the curtain slowly going up on a new and exciting part of my own particular story. Then the
management had suddenly and abruptly broken in upon
my excitement, interrupting my play and announcing
firmly that all plays come to an end. There was to be
only one performance of each story—the first was the
last. It might be a long play, but when it was over, it was
over. The scenery and props would be dismantled and
the lumber of experience, what could be salvaged, would
be pounded together again in different combinations for
the next play. For each beginning there would be an
end.

I had learned that there were two sides to every coin,
and that the coin would always be turned. That sorrow

would follow joy. Henceforth all pleasure would be touched with pain and all rejoicing with melancholy.

> Ay, in the very temple of Delight
> Veil'd Melancholy has her sovran shrine.
> Though seen of none save him whose strenuous tongue
> Can burst Joy's grape against his palate fine;
> His soul shall taste the sadness of her might,
> And be among her cloudy trophies hung.

We turned from the grave exhausted and went back to the big, quiet, empty house. It would be empty, too, for my mother in the spring—empty except for thirty-seven years of memories. A vast, dreary expanse of ordinary living lay before all of us.

"How about a hand of penny-ante?" asked Jack after dinner.

It was a stroke of genius. We had always played cards together, and the game that night drew eight sad and weary people back into a family. The tension relaxed and we began breathing. We were reaffirming our strength and beginning to live again. Since we could not refuse to live, we started again, as a family.

The next morning at breakfast I said, "Well, I'll go up to Hamilton and get my stuff."

"What are you talking about?" asked my mother sharply. "You'll do no such thing. Don't you think I'm old enough to take care of myself?"

Hunnie went back to Syracuse University, where she was in her first year, and I went back to Hamilton. We went under protest, but we went.

About a month later I began to awake from the daze

in which I had been living. It was in the middle of a
class in English literature. Mr. Johnston seldom lectured.
Instead, he plied us with very specific questions about
what we had read, in an attempt to make us think.
Among other things, we had read "The Wife of Usher's
Well," a grim Scottish ballad about the death of the
wife's three sons and their return home after death for
one night.

There lived a wife at Usher's well,
And a wealthy wife was she;
She had three stout and stalwart sons,
And sent them o'er the sea.

They hadna been a week from her,
A week but barely ane,
When word came to the carline wife
That her three sons were gane.

They hadna been a week from her,
A week but barely three,
When word came to the carline wife
That her sons she'd never see.

"I wish the wind may never cease,
Nor fashes in the flood,
Till my three sons come hame to me,
In earthly flesh and blood!"

It fell about the Martinmas,
When nights are lang and mirk,
The carline wife's three sons came hame,
And their hats were o' the birk.

It neither grew in syke nor ditch,
Nor yet in ony sheugh;
But at the gates o' Paradise
That birk grew fair eneugh.

"Blow up the fire, my maidens!
Bring water from the well!
For a' my house shall feast this night,
Since my three sons are well."

And she has made to them a bed,
She's made it large and wide;
And she's ta'en her mantle her about,
Sat down at the bed side.

Up then crew the red, red cock,
And up and crew the gray;
The eldest to the youngest said,
"Tis time we were away."

The cock he hadna craw'd but once,
And clapp'd his wings at a',
When the youngest to the eldest said,
"Brother, we must awa'."

"The cock doth craw, the day doth daw,
The channerin' worm doth chide;
Gin we be miss'd out o' our place,
A sair pain we maun bide."

"Lie still, lie still but a little wee while,
Lie still but if we may;
Gin my mother should miss us when she wakes,
She'll go mad ere it be day."

"Fare ye weel, my mother dear!
Fareweel to barn and byre!
And fare ye weel, the bonny lass
That kindles my mother's fire!"

"Why should one of the brothers say good-by to the servant?" Mr. Johnston asked. "It's easy to understand why he should mention his mother, but why the scullery maid?"

The question went around the room, but no one could give a plausible explanation.

"Maybe he was in love with the servant?" Mr. Johnston suggested, but no one could see any evidence for that in the ballad.

"Why should he mention her, then?" he repeated.

To my surprise, I suddenly found myself answering the question. "Because she was a familiar part of his home. Her lighting the fire every morning was simply a part of the routine of living in the place he had loved. She symbolized all the comfort and pleasure and security that home had meant for him."

I understood the son's longing for the familiar pattern of life at home—his need to reassure himself that the routine would go on and on forever like Coleridge's brook, "which to the woods all night singeth a quiet tune." Having succeeded, through the power of his desire, in seeing it all once more as it had been, here for the last time he bade it farewell.

I longed to revisit the home that had vanished. I would miss my father as a person, but as much as this, I would miss the pattern of our lives his presence shaped

—the smells of fried chicken and biscuits or glazed ham prickly with cloves, the smack of his evening newspaper, the brisk footsteps and the cheerful "hello," the evening kiss; the scratch of a match; and the bloom of cigar smoke filling the house. This was the quiet tune death had modulated into the minor so that it now rang strangely upon my ear.

I understood then that this ballad was about people, real people, people who lived and felt as I did, that, though the language seemed odd and was separated from me by thousands of miles and hundreds of years, it spoke to me directly about my own life and my own home. For the first time, I was deeply moved by a poem.

Until then I had studied poems as though they were collections of riddles to which I had to find prose answers in order to pass occasional exams. The exercise had been pleasant, but no poem, until this ballad, had touched the secret spring of my life. Restraint of emotion was part of our family's life, but my blindness had turned restraint into numbness. People were always being overcome by pity or sympathy or maudlin affection for blind children. I could not forget Freddy's mother. This emotionalism seemed to me to make fools of the adults and of the objects of their feelings. I reacted so strongly against these scenes that I had refused to acknowledge that I, too, possessed any feelings; that I, too, could feel deeply.

"The Wife of Usher's Well" taught me to feel, and this was the road that would lead me from the land of the white crow. Like the earth in winter, I had encased myself in an armor of frost to protect myself from the plowshare of experience; and, like the earth in winter, I had lain dormant, bringing forth no fruit. My father's death burned through, lighting the fuse of a slow internal explosion that shivered my armor. My spirit lay bare in the sunshine of spring. As Edith Sitwell says, "Death is the pain of becoming spring."

Soon I discovered my kinship with Wordsworth, the twilight wizardry of Coleridge enchanted me, and, under the careful tutelage of George Nesbitt and Tom Johnston at Hamilton, I felt myself expanding.

Poetry was the purest language of the human spirit, and, what was even more wonderful, I participated in that spirit. This proved I was *not* a white crow. I recognized as belonging to my own experience those sensations Wordsworth had felt. I knew what he meant by the "aching joys" of youth; I had known them all in the fields and on the river.

The human body—the fantastic mechanism registering, analyzing, interpreting, and recording those moments that are the mountaintops of life—this body must collapse and disintegrate, but this was not really death. Those moments, those mountaintops, remained. Wordsworth was not really dead, for his dreams and exaltations ran in blood along the heart.

Death was not really final, then. For Wordsworth, for my father, and even for me there was no real death; the sum and substance of a man was not confined to his flesh and blood. The real man existed in his dreams. The flesh might be mortal, but the man was not. He continued to live in the memory of his children, his nation, or, like Shakespeare, in the continuous mind of the race.

The great poets had simply taken the common, abiding experiences of all mankind and crystallized them. This was the discovery of my seventeenth year.

It followed quite naturally that the study of poetry was a study of the self. It was a descent into the pillared chamber of the human spirit in which I had so miraculously discovered that I, too, had a share. I had bought my ticket with grief.

Since all good poetry is about life, one must gain some knowledge of life before the poetry is meaningful. To meet death close by, to fall in love—then one may be ready to understand.

Death had plowed my desert, and I was beginning to understand.

That second year at Hamilton was far different from my first. Indeed, the whole atmosphere had changed, not only for me but for everyone. The adolescent gaiety of undergraduate life had been replaced by somber preparation. "Wait till the *sun* shines *Nelly*" rang out with the sound of marching feet, as long lines of uniformed men moved about the campus. Though we civilians wore sports jackets, our minds slipped into step with the firm rhythm. The whole college seemed in motion. Everyone was getting ready to go. Nobody knew where, but everybody knew he was going.

At dinner one night a friend of mine said half humorously, "I feel sorry for you, Russell. The Navy's lucky to get me, all right; but where are you going to find such a superb reader? Why, next year you'll have to hire some serviceman to read Browning to you. You'll be the only civilian on The Hill."

"No," I replied. "I'm not going to have any trouble finding readers. I won't be here."

"Where are you going? Into the WAACS?"

"Oh, I don't know; I'll transfer." The thought had just that moment occurred to me, but I tried to state my decision as though I had resolved upon it some months before. "I think I'll go . . ." and I reached for a name —"to . . . Yale."

"Aw, hell! You're kidding."

"No, I'm not," I said emphatically. My pride wouldn't let me abandon a position I had so whimsically taken, and I repeated, "I'm going to Yale."

"Have you applied?"

"Not yet, but I will."

I felt I had been guilty of a kind of impudence in having mentioned Yale so casually, but, having committed myself, I had to follow through—so I sent off a letter to New Haven.

By June of 1943 most of the civilians on the campus were gone. Graduation brought with it a wave of nostalgia. There were many mournful beer parties, much shaking of hands. Everyone was going into the services, everyone, that is, but me. However, I had won my right to feel miserable too, by having decided of my own free will to leave Hamilton. My decision had seemed to come on the spur of the moment, the result of only a whim, but gradually I realized this was not the case. For many weeks I had been making up my mind to go. I think I would have left even if there had been no wholesale drafting of my friends and even if I had not been caught up in the mood of departure.

I knew Hamilton too well. I liked it too well. I fitted in too well. It was too secure. I had to leave because I was afraid to leave; that was the real truth of the matter.

13. Pushing Streetcars

While waiting to hear from Yale, I looked for a summer job. I turned in my search to Mrs. Mary K. De Witt, the woman in charge of the Workshop for the Blind in Binghamton.

"All right," she said, "we'll give you a job. Have you ever worked a loom?"

"No, but I can learn."

I freely chose to throw a shuttle for forty hours a week to earn a wage equivalent to that of a part-time maid. This was pocket money for me. For some, it was a career. Out of such salaries they had to scrape the rent, shoes, and meals. Many of them were physically capable of doing any number of jobs in the Binghamton factories where they could have earned enough to live with some measure of decency. It was not their physical incapacity that kept them in poverty, but the public's view of it.

While I sensed the wall against which they battered their hearts, I cherished the smug illusion that it would never be an obstacle for me; that when the time came, with my college training, I could vault this barrier. But an incident took place that cast a shadow on this illusion.

One of the workers in the shop was a college graduate. He had some vision, but very little. Perhaps he, too, had gone to college fired by all the excitement I then felt and with dreams of forging a place for himself in the world of the sighted. Whatever his hopes and dreams had been, now they were crushed and his heart seared with bitterness. The springs of joy were dried up and choked with the acid truth that nowhere would anyone let him even compete for a chance to show what he could do.

Buoyed up by the courage and optimism of youth, he had flung himself into the struggle and had pitted his strength against the huge and impersonal machine of society. Everywhere he turned he met with the same rebuff, the unconditional rejection coated with the sugar of praise.

"Wonderful what you fellows can do! Simply wonderful. A college degree and everything. I don't see how you do it. I guess you fellows just have a little more of what it takes than the rest of us, but I'm afraid we don't have anything you can do."

The same people who refused him a future would, if

they had passed him on the street holding a tin cup, have thrown him a quarter.

It is an unwritten law that whoever shall constantly and openly receive charity from another shall lose his integrity and self-respect, and he shall hate him who has taken this away. It is indeed more blessed to give than to receive, and if a man is prevented from giving, he suffers the ultimate frustration.

But this is what society did to my colleague in the workshop. He had a mind carefully trained in special skills, and he was told by prospective sweet-tongued employers that they would under no circumstances let him use those skills. He was expected to withdraw gracefully, accepting their gift of praise, and quietly to weave pocketbooks for charitable buyers.

They dragged his body out of the Chenango River one cold, gray morning.

I was deeply shocked. But perhaps death in the cold Chenango was to be preferred to the living death of weaving pocketbooks behind the wall. I forced this misgiving back into a corner of my mind and piled new hopes on top of it, for a letter arrived announcing my acceptance at Yale with a scholarship.

During the war, Yale was not a gay place. The students were all young, and they worked furiously, going to summer school as well, in order to get their degrees before the draft got them. The spirit of friendship and conviviality that had reigned at the smaller Hamilton was nowhere to be found at Yale—at least not by a newcomer who entered as a junior. The accelerated program practically deprived the student of the sense of belonging to any particular class. I knew only Dike Ninninger, the reader whom the university had arranged for me, and my roommate, Ben. Ben worked twenty hours a day and slept the other four, and Dike, who also worked at the Faculty Club, had no time for relaxation either.

The classes I had so looked forward to were all lectures, and I never had a chance to speak to my instructors except to make special arrangements about examinations. Everyone was too busy even to say "hello." I went from class to class, from building to building, in silence. I passed outside the edges of conversations in the halls; I sat outside the edges of conversations at meals. I was alone.

The great university was in those first few weeks like a factory, and I was a single chunk of raw material being dragged along on a conveyor belt. As I lay at night listening to the traffic whirring and buzzing past my window, I wondered whether coming to Yale had not been a tragic mistake. It was too big, too impersonal, and I was too sensitive.

About this time I received a letter from the registrar at Hamilton wanting to know why I had transferred. Had I been unhappy there?

I sat down at my typewriter and hammered out a four-page reply that in substance was a comparison of Hamilton and Yale, by which Yale suffered severely. I mustered up all the youthful eloquence I could command and fumed and blasted the great university off the map. It seemed to me patently obvious that, since I was desperately unhappy at Yale, there must be something drastically wrong with the place. There could certainly be nothing wrong with me.

A week later, in reply to my bombastic answer, I received a note from the registrar accompanied by a mimeographed copy of my diatribe, which left my name and the name of Yale blank. The note requested my permission to use my letter in the Alumni Fund Drive. I was delighted. I was being published.

And, what's more, I had indirectly published a blow against the mechanism that ignored my individuality and was slowly grinding me into the dust. I felt I had struck back.

But this pleasure was short-lived. Suddenly it occurred to me that I might try wrestling. After all, it had worked miracles at Hamilton.

"Dike," I said one afternoon, "Yale has a wrestling team, doesn't it?"

"I suppose so. Why?"

"Will you show me where the gym is? I need some exercise."

"Let's finish this Wordsworth first, eh?"

"No! Damn Wordsworth! Come on." I went to my closet and pulled out the bundle of sweat clothes and my sneakers, and we trudged six blocks up Grove Street to the gym.

We entered a building so big the sound of our footsteps died away in the distance. It sounded to me like Grand Central Station.

"Hey, Dike; what are we doing here?"

"This is the gym. I'll take you to the elevator, and the guy there will take you to the wrestling room."

Elevator! This was a factory, all right. We walked for what seemed like fifty yards to where elevator doors rumbled and clashed.

"Hi, can you take this fellow to the wrestling room? See you later, Bob." Up we went to the sixth floor. The operator took me across the hall to an office and told me to wait. It all seemed preposterous. Elevators; sixth floors; offices. The only comforting thing was the familiar smell of rubbing alcohol and perspiration.

"Hey, Eddie! Eddie! Here's a guy wants to see you."

"Okay, Al," came a cheerful voice from the distance. Al went back to his elevator; the doors rumbled and clashed, and I was alone.

"Hello, boy," said the cheerful voice. "What do you want to see me about?"

"I wanted to see the wrestling coach," I explained. "I want to wrestle."

"I'm the wrestling coach. Eddie O'Donald's my name, but I'm afraid I can't let you wrestle. Wrestling's a tough sport, and we don't want to get anybody hurt, see. I'll get the elevator for you."

"Wait a minute," I objected, "I've wrestled before, and I want to wrestle now."

"You have? Have you ever heard of a half nelson? You see, it goes like this," and he started to slip an arm under mine from behind. I clamped down on his arm above the elbow and pretended to start a roll.

"Hey!" he cried, "that's all right. Take it easy, now. Sit down here."

"John," he shouted to his brother, the assistant coach, "come here a minute, will you? Here's a guy who can't see that says he wants to wrestle."

There were footsteps in the hall and a friendly voice in the doorway said, "Hello, boy. Do you think you can wrestle?"

"I've wrestled before," I repeated.

"Yeah, he's wrestled," interrupted Eddie. "I put a nelson on him and he started to roll me. What do you think?"

"But have you ever wrestled fellows who can see?" asked John.

"Sure."

"Well," said John, "if he wants to, let him have a shot."

"Okay, boy; put on your clothes and we'll see."

Quickly I undressed and got into my sweat clothes. They took me down the hall into a vast room whose floor and walls were completely covered with mats. It was filled with the scraping and thumping of many wrestlers.

"Hey, Pargsley," shouted Eddie, "come here a minute." Feet thudded across the mats. "Here, work with this guy a little and take it easy. He can't see."

Pargsley took it too easy.

"Did you see that!" Eddie muttered. "Okay, boy. What did you say your name was? You've wrestled before all right, and I guess you'll do."

For the next hour he put me through tests with several wrestlers, and, while I was dressing to go back for dinner, said, "Can you find your way up here tomorrow? We'd like to see some more of you."

That evening I went back to my college, Timothy Dwight, happier than I had been for weeks. I seemed to have convinced somebody of something, anyway. They wanted me to come back. And I did go back, every afternoon.

Wrestling didn't really solve the problem of meeting people, for on the mats there was no time to explore the possibilities of friendship. We were too interested in pinning one another. But the regular exercise of mind and body had its effect, purging me of some of my frustration. My good physical condition stood me in good stead at least once that fall.

I usually slept through breakfast and ate at a drugstore on the corner across Whitney Avenue. Whitney Avenue was a busy street, but crossing it offered no unusual difficulties. As I always did at corners where there were traffic lights, I simply waited until the cars began to move in the direction I wanted to go; then I could be certain there would be practically no cars moving along the street I wanted to cross. Sometimes, of course, drivers turned the corner on the red light, but that couldn't be helped. In this business one has to play the percentages.

I waited one morning on the corner of Grove and Whitney until the traffic began to move along Grove, and then I crossed Whitney. The drugstore was always easy to find because the entrance was directly opposite a manhole on the corner. I could hit that manhole every time without fail, step up onto the curb, and walk directly into the drugstore. I had made friends with the counter girls as well as with Louise, who managed the place. In fact, Louise often sat down and had a cup of coffee with me in the morning. This morning, however, my unerring aim for the manhole cover was a distinct disadvantage.

Almost to the curb, I kicked something—a rack with a red flag, as I learned later. It was light, so I brushed it casually out of my way. The next moment the earth opened beneath my feet and I was falling. Instinctively I spread my arms, though whether I actually hoped to catch something or merely to present a more graceful picture to the public as I disappeared I cannot say. Whatever my intention, I actually did catch the edge of the pavement. My sudden descent had so surprised me that for a moment I hung there suspended, collecting myself. Then, realizing this must be the sewer, I swung myself up, clambered out of the hole, and walked into the drugstore, where I ordered my coffee.

After a minute or two, Louise sat down beside me and wanted to know how I had got my shirt covered with dirt. She ordered a cup of coffee for herself, but before she had taken the first sip, the telephone rang. She jumped up to answer it and I heard her saying, "Hello . . . What? . . . You're kidding! . . . Oh, go on! You shouldn't drink at this time of day . . . No, I'm sorry; I haven't seen him. You're nuts. 'By." She hung up and came back to her coffee, laughing.

"You know what, Bob? Some one just called from down the street and said he saw some guy fall . . .

whoops! there's that phone again. Excuse me . . . Hello . . . yeah, now wait a minute! You're the second one. I don't know what you're talking about. . . . Someone else just called and said the same thing. Is this a game or something? No, he didn't come in here. Good-by." And she hung up the receiver, laughing even harder.

"Bob, that's the second one. He said he saw someone fall down the sewer outside, climb out, and stagger in here. I think they're all crazy. Nobody's come in since you've been here, have they?"

"No, not since I came in."

After a few moments two repairmen from the telephone company walked in to investigate. Louise was almost frantic.

"You can look down there, if you want to," she said. "Maybe he fell down and didn't get out. But whatever happened, he didn't come in here!"

"Bad luck for him if he didn't get out," said one of the men. "There's a twelve-thousand-volt cable bare down there. If he hit that, you can be sure he didn't get out."

"My God!" exclaimed Louise, and I spilled my coffee.

I said nothing about my adventure, so I was greatly surprised when, three days later, a representative from the Telephone Company called on me.

"We heard about your little accident the other day," he began in honeyed accents, "and I'm glad to see you're all right."

"How did you know?" I asked.

"There's a dentist whose office is over the drugstore. Apparently he's a regular at the morning coffee klatch, because he knows you. He happened to be looking out his window and he saw you fall in and climb out. You won't mind just signing these waivers, will you?" A fellow from across the hall wandered into my room at the time, and he pricked up his ears.

"Waivers!" he exclaimed, "waivers for what?"

"Well," simpered the telephone man, "for any damages, you know."

"He's not signing any waivers," cried my friend, assuming the role of my attorney. "Bob's been mighty brave about it, but none of us knows what he's been suffering. He wouldn't even let me bandage his arm or his head. His head! That's where he's really hurt. Why, he may not recover for years; maybe never. No, sir! We're going to sue for a hundred thousand."

"Now, just a minute, fellows," pleaded the telephone man. "We can talk this over quietly. Let's not get upset, shall we?"

My friend turned to me and asked, "What the hell happened, anyway, Bob?" The telephone man breathed a deep sigh of relief. "Nothing at all," he reassured my friend, "just a little mishap not really worth mentioning, but you know how it is. The company likes to have things settled, sort of." Then the whole story came out, much to my friend's amusement, and I signed the waivers.

I walked the six blocks up to the gym at four-thirty every afternoon and came back for dinner at six-fifteen. One damp, cold evening in late November I was walking back as usual. The streets I had to cross were all quiet except College Street, which boasted a trolley line as well as a good deal of traffic. Whenever I heard a trolley approaching I let it grind past until it was far down the street before I crossed, for it was impossible to hear an automobile above the trolley's screech and rumble. This night, however, it lumbered along College and stopped at the intersection where I stood. I was later than usual and did not want to miss dinner, and the trolley seemed to have no intention of moving on. I stepped off the curb and marched out into the intersection, making a wide swing into Grove Street to pass in front of it.

I never carried a cane at Yale, which explains what happened at the moment I passed directly in front of the trolley. With a sudden groan it moved down upon me. It nuzzled my right shoulder like a dinosaur. In sudden anger I turned upon it, set my shoulder against the steel, dug my heels into the slush on the street, and shoved with all my might.

The conductor probably never realized I was blind; he undoubtedly thought me drunk or just plain crazy. He reversed the car with a "wow, wow, wow" of profanity from somewhere inside the cavernous stomach of the beast, and it retreated with a mechanical hiccup. I crossed to the opposite curb and went on to dinner.

Pushing the streetcar was not something I thought about doing. If I had thought about anything at that moment, it would certainly have been how to get out of its way. Pitting my body against the machine was an act that sprang solely from my attitude of mind, a sudden refusal to be moved from my path by anything, not even a streetcar. The big, impersonal mechanism became a symbol of the big, impersonal university.

My defiance and pigheadedness on this occasion marked a change in my attitude toward my life at Yale. I would not be ground under; I would not spend my days in lamenting the lost security of Hamilton and all my friends; I would be damned if I was going to confess my own weakness. I would push and push and push.

I was shooting for a place on the Yale wrestling varsity as its 165-pounder. This spot was held down by the captain, but since I beat him regularly in the daily workouts, my hopes were high. The publicity director got wind of my wrestling and the New Haven papers began carrying wild stories about me.

NEW BLIND SENSATION ON MATS

BLIND WRESTLER CRUSHES

OPPONENTS

A reliable spokesman for the University declares that Yale will have an intercollegiate champion on its squad this coming year, Bob Russell, the blind tornado.

But on the day of our first meet with West Point the sports pages were dramatically silent. Two days before the meet, in an easy elimination bout after which I could have challenged the captain, I tore a ligament in my shoulder. The publicity build-up had fizzled out.

In a month I had recovered enough for an easy workout.

"Take it easy, boy," cautioned Eddie O'Donald, "I'm going to use you Saturday against Columbia."

"When do I wrestle the elminations?"

"No eliminations for you. Gene's got a skin infection so he's sidelined."

The sports pages blared out all they had had to withhold a month earlier. *Time* Magazine sent a reporter and a photographer to cover my bout. The next week's issue carried the story of my victory over the Columbia man.

The following Monday afternoon I was amazed to find Gene miraculously recovered. That proved to be a bad afternoon, for I sprained an ankle so badly I hobbled around with a heavy cane for the rest of the season. The "tornado" had passed, and the sports pages were dead calm.

Though *Time* had a large circulation, the effect, so far as I was concerned, was a limited one—limited, in fact, to my roommate Ben, who came bashfully into my bedroom with his copy of the magazine to ask for my autograph.

Ben was an engineer and a crack mathematician who worked so hard that he put me to shame. He spent eight hours a day slogging at his books and jiggling his slide rule, after which he took a turn around the quadrangle for relaxation and returned for three or four more hours of study before bed. He was a constant inspiration to me, but, like all admirable people, he made me embarrassed by my own laziness. When exams rolled around at the end of that first semester, I said to him, "Ben, take it easy. The best preparation for an exam is a good night's sleep. In order to sleep, one must relax, and the best way to relax is by playing a few hands of cards. I have a deck right here. Let me teach you the rudiments of poker."

Ben sat down reluctantly but soon became a willing pupil. After a few minutes he seemed to be catching on, so I explained further that, though it was not really necessary, most people, just to make it more interesting, usually played the game for money, wagering a penny or two now and then. Ben obediently reached into his pocket and drew forth a handful of change.

"All right," he said, "how do you bet?"

The walls of Timothy Dwight are thick and the rooms nearly soundproof. The moving of heavy furniture and even an occasional brisk free-for-all seldom arouse much interest or curiosity, but the chink of small coins on a wooden table and the soft whisper of rustling pasteboards can be heard anywhere in the college. Before long a stream of curious and nervous stragglers begin to appear like so many sheepish bloodhounds who are not really sure this is the proper time for hunting. We had not played three hands before there was a knock on the door and a contingent from across the hall drifted in and stood watching until invited to draw up chairs.

The game wandered on into the small hours, and, as I had promised him, when Ben got to bed he was so tired he slept like a child. He had good reason, too, for he had collected a tidy pile of gold before we quit. He was an apt scholar and took to the game with such energy and imagination that he soon outstripped his mentor.

I went to New York quite often that first year at Yale. I went largely to have something to do and also because it was, in a small way, an adventure every time. The Merritt Parkway passes near New Haven, and a twenty-cent bus ride takes you out to one of the entrances. Hitchhiking always had an element of romance for me, and this was increased tenfold when I hitchhiked alone.

Though I carried no cane, I never had any trouble getting cars to stop, but when I fumbled for the door handles most drivers usually suspected me of being drunk. When they did realize I was blind and not drunk, their reactions were almost identical. The questions began with, "Do you live in New Haven?"

"No, I live in Binghamton, a smallish place in central New York State."

"What are you doing in New Haven then?"

"I'm going to school there." This always stumped them for a moment while they tried hard to remember having heard of some funny sort of school being in New Haven. Finally they asked, "What school is that?"

"Yale."

After a pause one of them would usually ask, "You mean you're under observation there or something?"

"No," I would correct them, "I'm a student there." This usually ended the questioning: if I was going to lie about myself, there was no point in going on.

These junkets to New York were neither particularly wild nor gay; they did, however, use up the week ends. But, as my first year at Yale passed the halfway mark, I went to New York less and less. I was making more friends and finding things to do at Timothy Dwight. I came to know two law students, Ailey Allen and Nick Goodspeed, both of whom were freshmen counselors in

my college. They had been undergraduates at Yale before the war, and they had about them an easy grace
and quiet assurance. They possessed vigor of intellect as
well as unaffected modesty, combining the virtues of the
mind with those of social grace. In a word, they were
cultured. An invitation from them for sherry before dinner took the place of an invitation to a beer party from
a Hamilton fraternity. As the sherry replaced the beer,
so the pleasure of conversation replaced for me the
boisterous conviviality of Hamilton.

For us the luxuries of life had been dispensed with:
the white-coated waiters had disappeared from the dining halls; fraternities and secret societies retreated into
the shadowy corners of concern; and young men in
Brooks Brothers suits no longer swept about New Haven
in shiny convertibles. In their place surged a tide of non-
descript boys with worried expressions, riding rusty bi-
cycles and laden with books.

We wartime students were, for the most part, barbar-
ians, possessing all the vigor, independence, and determination of the uncivilized. Only a trickle of prep-
school graduates came into our ranks. Some tried to
preserve the old traditions. Others, like Ailey Allen and
Nick Goodspeed, preserved what was best—scholarship
with grace.

While walking back from a bridge game with Ailey
one night, I discovered I was out of tobacco.

"We'll drop into the Lizzie and get some," said Ailey.

"What or who is the Lizzie?" I asked.

"It's a club," he said simply. "Come on; here we are,"
and we turned into a small house on College Street. He

led me into the large, comfortably furnished living room and showed me the big rack of clay pipes with the humidor beneath. While I filled my pipe, Ailey disappeared into the kitchen and returned with two bottles of beer.

"Let's sit down for a minute."

I took my beer and we settled ourselves at a table.

"Tell me something about this place. I've never heard of it before."

"It's a club made up of undergraduates, graduates, and faculty. There's nothing secret about it. It's just a place where the members drop in for tea in the afternoon if they like. It's open in the evenings, too, and there's usually some beer in the refrigerator. It's a good quiet place to work. There's a marvelous library upstairs, and down here a vault of rare books, a priceless collection, really. In a small way it's a center for Elizabethan scholars. Your major is English, isn't it? Wouldn't you like to join?"

"I certainly would," I replied, "but I imagine it's too expensive."

"Six dollars a year, that's all. Alexander Smith, a big rug manufacturer, gave the club to the university, and it operates largely on his endowment. The only thing we pay for is our beers or Cokes. I'll put you up for membership, if you like, and Nick will second you."

I was surprised and very pleased when, a few weeks later, I received a notice informing me I had been elected to the Elizabethan Club. I went to tea that very afternoon with Nick and soon became an habitué.

It was a wonderful place, where students and faculty

met in an atmosphere of friendship and where there was no barrier separating the lecturer from the listener. As a student at a huge university, I had a rare opportunity in the Elizabethan Club, and I exploited it to the full. I, and all the other members, past and present, owe a deep debt to Alexander Smith.

During my first semester in New Haven I had been *at* Yale; in my second semester I was *in* Yale. After a quiet tea at the Lizzie I reflected with shame that this was the very Yale against which, several months earlier, I had set an angry shoulder. The Lizzie wasn't something to be pushed; it couldn't be pushed. You couldn't push or fight your way into it any more than you could force your way into Catholicism by beating up a priest. I had been a fool, really. The thing to do with a streetcar was not to push it, but to get aboard.

14. Looking for the Obvious

The choice of how to make one's living is crucial, for the work a man does makes him what he will become. The blacksmith pounds the anvil, but the anvil also pounds the blacksmith. The clam's shell turns golden in the brown depths of the ocean, and in far more subtle ways is a man's mind colored by the course of his life. So when a man chooses his labor, he chooses his future self.

Could I, for example, go into industry after graduating and work my way "up to something"? I really knew nothing about the demands such a life would make upon me, and I had no idea what the effects of that sort of life would be. It seemed sensible to try working in a factory. The pay would be good.

In Endicott, about ten miles from Binghamton, International Business Machines has a large plant, so soon after I returned home from my junior year I took a bus to the plant and explained to the personnel man that I wanted a summer job.

In cooperation with Mrs. De Witt and the Binghamton Lions Club, sponsor of the Binghamton Workshop for the Blind, I.B.M. had hired Michael Supa, a young man who had been blind almost since birth and who had just graduated from Colgate. He had gone into I.B.M. with the intention of trying to perform every operation in the plant, after which he could tell management which jobs could be performed competently by people without sight. After he had finished his survey, he began working with Mrs. De Witt, gradually siphoning off workers from the Workshop for the Blind and placing them in the I.B.M. plant.

There were then only a few blind people working at I.B.M.; nevertheless, the ice had been broken and the personnel department received my application without raised eyebrows or patronizing smiles. I was given a job in the "tabbing department," ten hours a day, five days a week, for seventy cents an hour. I was to begin the following Monday.

When Monday came, I jumped out of bed at six, made my own breakfast, grabbed my bag of sandwiches from the refrigerator, and walked to the corner, where I caught a bus for work. My excitement and enthusiasm refused to be dampened by the busload of silent, sleepy, and morose passengers headed for the same destination.

"Over here," called a voice from one of the gates in the fence surrounding I.B.M. "Are you the new guy? Okay, come on; got your pass to show the guard?" And I was inside, being taken to my bench.

"I'm the Assistant Foreman," said the man as he led me along. "Here's your bench. Now I'll show you your job."

My work was simple. Anyone who has ever punched a time clock will understand just how simple. I.B.M. makes a very fine time clock, and it also makes racks to hold the time cards. These racks were made in the section of the plant in which I worked. When the rack came to me, it was all finished except for my operation. Each rack was about four inches wide and two and a half feet long, with twenty-five slots, each of which would hold a time card. Above each of these large slots was a smaller one, and it was my job to slip a tiny piece of cardboard into each one. On this bit of cardboard or tab was to be written the number of the time card belonging in the larger slot beneath. Once I had developed a technique and a rhythm, the operation took about one second to perform. So for ten hours every day, five days a week, I slipped tabs into time-card racks. After the first million or so, my enthusiasm began to flag.

The first week was all right because I was interested in everyone about me and in the task of developing my own technique for the operation. The other people doing the same job finished between 140 and 180 racks every day. The first day I managed 90, the second, 120;

145 on Wednesday, 180 on Thursday, and 200 on Friday. My progress gave me pleasure and I enjoyed talking to other people. The high point of the second week occurred when I received my check for the first week's work. But after that I entered upon the desert of monotony known only to the factory worker.

There was really nothing to work toward. As a summer worker, I was not eligible for a raise; so the only goal I had to shoot at was to break my own production record. Once having done that, I set about breaking the new one. This was not without its repercussions, for my co-workers soon became annoyed by my doing so much work. It was not as if they couldn't have kept pace with me if they had wanted to. They didn't want to. Yet, if they did not speed up, they were liable to be accused of being lazy when a newcomer, and a blind one at that, came and produced more than they did. I was soon dubbed a "job killer," an expression I had never really understood until then.

I received lessons in how to sit still without doing anything, but that was worse than working. I had no desire of being a thorn in anyone's side, nor did I want to show anyone up. It was simply less trouble to work than not to work.

When I finished a rack, I stood it at the end of my bench with the others. I began to take a fanatic pride in the rows of finished racks extending out into the aisle. I lined them up evenly, made certain they all stood straight, and gradually built up battalions and regiments of soldiers, each of which stood in full dress and always at attention. The objective was to send out my troops, to advance, to storm, and to overwhelm my neighbor's bench.

The archenemy was the Assistant Foreman. When my men began to creep stealthily out into the aisle, when I had forty or fifty standing in perfect lines and beginning to stretch toward the opposite bench, I worked with a fury approaching panic. I knew that once my tactics were discovered, once I was found out, it would all be up with me, for he would come with his handcart and sweep my men from the field in wholesale slaughter.

When my forces swelled to fifty, my heart began to palpitate and my fingers twitched with excitement. Could I make fifty-five? Oh, God, just five more!

"Hey, George," someone called, "come here a minute, will you?" And the sleepy voice of the Assistant Foreman answered, "Yeah, what do you want, Joe?"

I sighed with relief. He would be busy for another few minutes, and I worked furiously in silence. Fifty-five . . . sixty! . . . A few more; just a few more! Seventy would be too much to hope for, but could I make sixty-five? I began to secrete small squads on my right and brought them out of hiding only when I felt I must certainly be discovered. Sixty-five! Sixty-six, seven, eight. I might make seventy, and I had calculated it would take only about eighty. I might . . . sixty-nine . . . really succeed.

Crash! And my vanguard collapsed in a heap on the handcart.

"Hey, Bob; what are you doing here? You're blocking the aisle," said the sleepy voice. My heart sank and a small spot of hot rage glowed deep inside. Like Sisyphus of old, I was condemned to an impossible task.

I played other games, too: trying, for example, to imagine the state of mind Coleridge was in when he created "Kubla Khan" or distilled it or wrote it or copied it from memory. I tried to cut the moorings of the balloon of my own mind and at the same time keep one bit of me on earth to see in which direction the winds of fancy would take it. It rose slowly at first, struggling, as it were, to find the current of association through which to escape. But as it rose, it gained speed until at last it was fairly bouncing this way and that about the sky, beyond control. With increasing difficulty, I retrieved it to examine the impressions it had taken during its reckless flight. Alas, my "Kubla Khan" was not inside—not a single line of poetry or one coherent thought. I tried more flights, because while my mind was absent, the hands of the clock fairly spun around. Indeed, these flights became habitual, though each time it was harder to get back to reality.

I had intended to do plenty of important reading that summer. For example, I had *The Divine Comedy* on Talking Book Records.

I strove to concentrate, but my mind was a flabby bag that bellied and flapped in the wind. It was hopeless. I sent Dante back to the library and ordered *Cappy Ricks Returns.* I could follow the story, but that was all. Fortunately, that's all there was. To cut the moorings of the intellect when I entered the factory at seven and to retrieve it just before quitting time at six had become more than just a game; it had become a drug and I, an addict.

"So you're thinking of teaching, are you?" asked Mr. Mendell at the Lizzie one afternoon when I had returned to Yale. Though he was a professor of history and I had never taken any courses from him, we met frequently at the Elizabethan Club and often talked together.

"Yes," I replied, "I think I would like to teach."

"You had better do more than *think* so," he continued, "because it's going to be no easy business. I suppose you will want to teach in a school for the blind?"

"No, of course not!" I answered. The idea had never occurred to me. "I want to teach in a college." He didn't laugh, but only because he was too kind.

"Do you know what you are saying?" he went on. "That'll mean several more years of graduate work, which is extremely expensive, apart from being all but impossible for you. I don't see how . . . well, for example, I gave one of my graduate students a little project to work on that will probably necessitate his looking at a hundred or a hundred and twenty-five books in the library. Of course, he won't have to read all those, but he will have to look through them to see if they contain anything pertinent to his subject. Now, how are you going to do anything like that?"

"I don't know," I said with a sinking feeling.

"And even if you could, how could you make all the notes on those books; footnotes, bibliographies, and so on? You can't carry a Braillewriter along with you through the library stacks. What kind of filing system can you use for those huge, cumbersome notes? And besides, the pace at which you must work is infinitely slower than that of anyone who can see. Perhaps in the course of a few months, with the devoted help of several readers and a hundred pounds of Braille paper, you could produce a paper like the one I want from this student of mine, but he has only ten days in which to do it. He'll have to do several papers of this sort before he even has the right to embark on a thesis for his degree. And a thesis! Well, that's quite out of the question.

"I'm not trying to discourage you," he continued, "but just face it squarely now. For the sake of argument, let's suppose you have done all this, have your degree, and so on. How do you think you're going to get a job? Who'll give you a chance when there will probably be ten people with sight applying for the same job? And if somebody did give you a job, your advancement in teaching at the college level depends almost completely on the scholarly articles you must write for learned journals. You will have your hands more than full just with teaching. If you are to hope for promotion, especially in those early years, you have to produce. I just don't see how you can.

"And suppose you do. Your salary will be minute. What will you have gained after four or five more years? You would probably earn just as much, have a much easier road to advancement, and, what's more, make a more significant contribution to other people if you returned to a school for the blind to teach there. If you were playing stud poker, you wouldn't play your hand without looking at the hole card, would you? In educational circles for the blind, that card is an ace for you. Otherwise, well, I don't see how . . ."

I left the Lizzie that afternoon in utter dejection. I was certain Mr. Mendell had spoken the complete truth. He was telling me honestly what he thought I should know. However, he did not know, he could never know, what it would mean to me to go back behind the fence. In the three years that had passed since leaving the Institute, I had quite forgotten about the fence, but now once more I could hear the clang of the gate.

A few days later I went to see Professor Chauncey Tinker, a man whose wisdom and scholarship had won for him an international reputation and whose skill as a teacher always made his courses among the most popular on the campus. His many kindnesses to me had encouraged me to speak openly to him of my deep frustration because of the impenetrable screen standing between me and the miles of books in the library—of that black fury that descended upon me in waves, like malaria, when I realized again the vastness of literature and of my huge and passionate hunger to devour it. I felt like some strange beast tethered by a malignant deity at the gates of paradise, just inside which there grew fruits whose sweetness, I knew, surpassed my wildest imaginings. And this god, this devil, tossed an occasional morsel over the wall so he might have the sport of watching the poor beast bolt it with ravenous greed, a morsel never large enough to satisfy, but only to excite greater hunger.

To my surprise, Professor Tinker understood my feelings far better than I expected. In his ninth year his vision had been impaired by an accident, and he had been forced since then to protect his remaining sight. This meant that, although he could read, he, too, could never give free rein to his appetite.

What I wanted from Professor Tinker was not pity, but his honest opinion—could I make a go of it as a teacher of literature? He told me of a Professor Paul Mueschke at the University of Michigan who was blind, but whose learning and scholarship he respected profoundly. This was high praise indeed.

"I can't think how he has done it. It is utterly beyond me, my boy, but it should mean something to you that there is one man at least who has done what you want to do. If I were to speak from my own knowledge of your difficulties and what must inevitably lie before you, I would say no, you cannot hope for success. But, then, you see, there is Professor Mueschke who has done it. So who am I to say whether you can or cannot? If you try it, you must reconcile yourself to the fact that you cannot be second-rate—you must be better than most before you will get even a fair chance. To tell you this, I suppose, is to tell you nothing. But if poetry means to you what I think it does, what else can you do but try? May God be with you."

Whether he had intended to encourage or dissuade me, I left Professor Tinker's office in the library knowing I must try. Talking to him made it plain there was no choice. I had been searching for the obvious.

I walked up to the gymnasium that afternoon not with iron resolution in my heart, but simply with my mind at rest. The large room was unusually crowded, but I had long since become accustomed to a push or a kick from the other grapplers. That afternoon it was my job to work out with our new manager, a novice at the sport. I had to show him some of the more common holds.

We were working out together very slowly and carefully when suddenly I was kicked on my ear by a wrestler nearby. The blow dazed me for a moment. When I recovered, I found I could hear almost nothing. The whole room had suddenly changed from a place whose every peculiarity I knew into a chaos of shouting and thuds. I could no longer tell direction or distance. At that moment, I knew what it was to fear. The manager led me through the jungle of arms and legs, out the door, and downstairs to the locker room.

After dressing, we went to the health department where one of the doctors examined me.

"Nothing serious, I think," he said reassuringly. "I'll just put in this oil and plug up your ears." This from miles away.

"But you can't do that," I exclaimed. "How am I to get around if you put plugs in my ears?"

"Oh, this will only be for a few days."

I sat quietly until he had finished, until he had sealed me off, and then let myself be led back to my dormitory, where, once alone, I carefully removed the plugs and at least regained partial communion with the world. But he had spoken the truth. In a few days I had quite recovered my hearing, and I was troubled by only occasional headaches and a ringing in my ears.

But for those few days I felt like a driver whose windshield is permanently covered with white mist. Accidents were inevitable. When I walked down the street I bumped into old landmarks I hadn't scraped in more than a year. I ran into people who stood chatting with each other at street corners, and each time I stepped off a curb it was an act of faith.

During those days I resolved never to wrestle again. Fear had prompted the decision, but there were also sound arguments to back it up. What Professor Tinker had said was perfectly true. My academic record had to be as good as I could make it. Those two hours every afternoon at the gym could and would be spent much more profitably with my readers.

Giving up wrestling was hard. I loved the sport, and it had done very well by me. It had helped to make a place for me at Hamilton, and it had won considerable recognition for me at Yale, and I was no more averse to recognition and acclaim than any other boy of nineteen. Still, it would have to go. There was too much at stake.

15. Mary and Faith

During the week of finals in my junior year, I sat at dinner one night with one of my readers, Kendall Mitchell, whose taste for the bizarre often took extravagant turns both in action and language. Suddenly he said, "It's all over now. Let's shake the dust from our feet and follow the Student Christian Movement to Sebago Lake for the Conference of New England Colleges."

"Can anyone go?" I asked.

"Anyone can be a Christian," he prompted; "even you, Robert."

"But what is this conference? What do people do up there?"

"It's coeducational," he said.

So Friday morning we boarded the train for Maine.

The conference site was a Boy Scout camp surrounded by a pine forest. There were about a hundred and fifty students from colleges all over New England, and we were housed in small cabins on the lake front. Ken and I shared one with four other fellows and, after arranging our stuff, we all went up to the lodge to find out the week's schedule.

We were told there would be a speaker each morning, usually a professor from a divinity school. He would be followed by an hour's silence for meditation, after which we would convene in small groups for discussion. The afternoons were planned for us, too. In the evenings there would be jolly community sings and movies. Curfew would be sounded at ten.

The week stretched before me like an interminable obstacle course. I was about to say something rude about the prospect to Ken when he escaped with, "Don't move, Robert; I forgot to pull up the drawbridge. Wait for me here at the lodge until I come back."

"What are you talking about?"

"I forgot to lock the cabin door. I, for one, don't trust these Christians; they have a lean and hungry look. I shall return." And he was gone.

Damn that Ken, anyway. Well, there was always the lake. I might borrow a rod and settle myself on a rock and wait for the salmon. Sebago was famous for its salmon, and at that very moment I could imagine a vast fish sliding out of the shadows. It was a beauty. It seemed to be making a pass at my bait when a voice at my elbow startled me.

"Hello, I'm Mary from Bates College."

"Oh!" I said, rousing myself and waving the salmon out of my thoughts. "Hello, I'm Bob from Yale."

"It's a nice place," I continued warily.

"Yes, very nice," came an equally cautious reply.

"It's interesting already. I mean the conference," I faltered, "that'll be interesting."

"Yes." She hesitated. "It will be a sort of change."

"A change? Yes," I agreed hastily, "a kind of vacation."

"Exactly; a vacation," she agreed.

"Here's your list of topics for possible discussion," intoned the grave voice of the clergyman in charge of the conference. He laid a sheaf of mimeographed pages on my lap. "We hope everyone will consider the list carefully before dinner and mark those he feels are particularly interesting. The lists will be collected after the evening meal," and he left.

Mary fell silent as she took her list, and I began to fear she would retreat to her cabin to actually consider the topics. After rustling the loose pages for a moment she said, "Very good. I think they're all very good topics and everyone ought to consider them very carefully. Shall we go swimming?"

She wasn't going to try to convert me, then. The sun came out again from behind the obstacle course.

"Well . . . yes," I said hesitantly.

"What's the name of your cabin?" she asked, sensing my embarrassment.

"Redwood."

"Come on then," she said. "We'd better hurry or we

won't have time for a dip before dinner." And taking my arm, she walked with me along the maze of rough trails to my cabin.

"I'll come back for you when I'm ready. Just wait outside here, okay?" and she ran off.

"Have you considered your topics?" asked a sepulchral voice from the corner, "You have not. I know all. Your mind has been occupied with earthly things."

"Ken," I began, "where the . . ."

"Now, now!" he corrected, "I went back to the lodge and found you engaged, so I slipped back here to brood over my list as you should have been doing. Instead of which you were frittering away the afternoon with that winsome wench. Shame, oh shame!"

"You devil," I cried, "you haven't been looking at any topics. You probably thought this was a good chance to scan the field." I changed into my trunks and stepped outside.

"Hello," Mary called. "Come on," and we went down to the lake. The water was icy, stinging our flesh into fierce exhilaration. We dived and swam and splashed for twenty minutes, after which we sat shivering and excited on the shore.

During the week that followed, Mary and I were seldom apart. We listened together to some of the morning speakers, but in the hours of meditation, we did not meditate. We planned our own afternoons and studiously avoided the jolly community sings and blaring movies. For us there was no curfew—only the soft evenings filled with the sound of crickets and frogs, and ever and always the bittersweet smell of the pines.

As we walked arm in arm along an old wagon track through the forest, I could feel the rhythmic swaying of her body. My heart began to pound. It seemed harder to breathe. Gradually I slowed my pace. In fear I waited for the forward pressure of her arm that would mean she understood, that she was saying, "No!"

The pressure did not come. She adjusted her pace to mine, till, finally, we stood still. A long moment of silence passed between us. I slipped my arm about her waist. Gently she leaned on my shoulder. Another moment of terror and joy, and then I drew her to me. She was real; she was alive; and she cared.

Shyly she turned away. I let her turn, still keeping my arm about her shoulder.

I was elated. Another gate had opened.

In the summer following the conference we wrote to each other almost daily. In August, when she graduated from Bates, she moved to New York with two other girls. They took a small apartment on the East Side, and I went down to spend almost every week end there.

Mary had a passion for economics and politics. She was always writing to her representatives in Congress about something, and when she could afford a telegram, she sent one. She was a good citizen.

"But don't you care about the steel industry?" she would say in amazement.

"Well, yes, of course I do," I would answer weakly.

"It's the backbone of this nation, and while it is in the hands of profiteers who bleed the workers, the country is deprived of initiative, strength, and social justice.

Don't you care about that? Don't you want to do something?"

"Yes," I stammered. It was like trying to argue with a preacher. You had to take the position that sin was a good thing, or else agree. I was part of the backbone of the indifferent masses. I was heartily ashamed of myself on Saturdays and Sundays, but when I returned to Yale and to reading Melville or Keats I forgot my shame.

I didn't dare take both my suits to New York, for she would have taken one and sent it to Spain. She was not above ferreting about in the closet I used and dragging out those old things with which squirrels like me can't part.

"You don't want this any more, do you?"

"Yes, I do. Put it back."

"But you never wear it!"

"I do wear it—that is, I will. It's a very good jacket. It was my brother's when he went to college, and he bought it when you could get really good material. Feel that stuff. The elbow can easily be stitched up. Now, just put it back."

But I soon discovered that her active social conscience was overpowering. What had drawn us together and held us was the silver chain of sex, whose links we followed with growing excitement. Fearful and tentative advances met with exquisitely shy withdrawal, until each discovered the basic truth about himself. The cool, rolling gold of her femininity gradually melted under my masculine touch. She was a woman; I was a man.

Of the importance of her discovery about herself I cannot speak. My discovery, for me, was crucial. The seeds of the wild hope that Adele had planted in me years before, Mary nourished and tended. The terrible fear that I was a shameful creature unmanned, almost dehumanized by blindness, she dispelled. Through poetry, I rejoined the race; through her, I became a man.

There had been other girls, of course—those dates at Hamilton, for example. But they were dates rather than people. For me they had been only part of social occasions. With Mary I needed neither alcohol nor music, two things I then thought essential when venturing out for an evening with a girl.

I never felt about Mary as I had felt about other girls; she was never a public charge nominally belonging to me. She never waited for someone to get her an ash tray; if she smoked, she went and got one and put it where we could both use it. She never waited for other people to do things for her, so my inability to do them was not borne in upon me.

She neither looked upon me as some sort of invalid who needed to be taken care of nor as a semi-supernatural being with powers verging on the miraculous. She looked upon me simply as a person.

When I told her I had hitchhiked she merely said, "Oh, good. How many rides did it take you?"

It was this more than anything else that first drew me to her. But this is not to love.

This magic comes only after both are touched by the wand of faery.

Soon I actually did fall in love. Faith also came from Binghamton, and was then attending Smith. We had known each other's names for several years, but we had probably not exchanged more than ten sentences until we happened to meet at a student conference in February, 1945.

After one of the meetings, we spent the rest of the evening together just talking. We never mentioned the steel industry. Faith's voice was soft and low, "an excellent thing in woman." She was quiet, unaffected, and there was something fresh and wonderful about her. I liked her. I liked her very much. In the days that followed, shadows began to gather about my image of Mary and I found it hard to recollect the sound of her voice. I began to feel guilty about her.

In March I invited Faith down to Yale for the Senior Prom. There must have been other people in New Haven that week end. I don't suppose the orchestra had been hired to play only for us, but we were alone in the confusion of clinking glasses, the swagger, and the laughter. We spoke only of things that mattered, and discovered that with each new confession we were confessing the other's faith, the other's devotion.

"And do you really feel that way? Oh, I'm glad! I feel the same way. I can't help telling you, even though it sounds silly."

"Yes, yes, I know. It's odd, isn't it, but suddenly it's tremendously important to tell only what's really true."

"Yes, it is odd, but then it isn't, really. Somehow it's right."

During the weeks that followed, I drifted away from

the shores of conventional life onto a planet where there were only the two of us. Never before had there been such a spring. The first crow went winging over the mountain, and on the strong beat of his wings and his shouts of raucous joy he carried the magic of rebirth.

For us there were long, delicious walks through the countryside around Northampton, and we lingered along the edges of Paradise Pond, whose placid waters formed the foundation of the house we built there, a house of wishes.

"And we shall live here together, do you think, in this house?"

"Yes, I think we shall. I think it is the only house where we shall ever really live, and it will always be the same for us."

"But will it always be the same? Sometimes I'm not very sure, and I would like always to be sure."

"When you're not sure, come down here to Paradise where we have built our house, and remember the wishes that made it and the hopes that sealed the corners, and remember we agreed never to put a roof on it because it is really only the beginning, and we shall have to build many stories yet. Putting the roof on is for God alone, and we must never forget to keep growing until He says, 'Enough.' "

And as the twilight and shadows began to sift gently down, the fierce little flame of ego, the tiny light that is the substance of the self, grew and softened until it became a part of the twilight. And with this softening, self and the awareness of self reached up and flowed out until being was everywhere and self was everything.

"And Place was where the Presence was
Circumference between."

The squeaking and lurching of the train and the im-
patient panting and grumpy cough of the little engine
yanking me back to New Haven on Sunday nights also
yanked me back to ordinary life and the ordinary way
it must be lived. With a sigh, I realized there probably
would be more unanswered letters from Mary waiting
for me. She had to be told. And with the heartlessness
only someone in love can show, I wrote and told her.

Faith graduated about three weeks before my final
examinations, and I spent a day with her at Northampton before she went back to Binghamton.

"It won't be long," I said. "I shall be home soon."

"Please hurry." Her first letter from home came to me
the following week, and she asked me to come to Binghamton that week end. I wrote I would come as soon as
I could, but I must work very hard for the exams,
which were only a few days off. Her answer came:

"Frank came home a few days ago. He was just released
from the Army, and he stopped in to say hello. He has
been staying here for a week now, and we are very deeply
in love. Do try to understand . . ."

Angry, proud, resentful, and in love, I packed my
suitcase and took the next train home. In a cloud of
smoke and the hiss of escaping steam, the conductor in
his matter-of-fact way slowly read through the familiar
catalogue of stations. Other passengers in flat, unemo-

tional voices chatted about the weather and their pleasure in seeing Ruthie again. Had Ruthie ever been in love? I doubted it. What the hell did Ruthie know about it? What did anybody know about it?

"*Bing*hamton, Bingham*ton*," called the conductor.

I phoned Faith from a booth at the station and arranged to have lunch with her at a restaurant I knew would be almost empty.

I was in luck. The restaurant was empty. Faith and I had the place to ourselves except for the waitress, and she spent her time in the kitchen.

I pleaded with Faith; I browbeat her; I told her it would be the greatest mistake of her life.

"You can't be sure!" I urged.

"No," she said quietly, "I'm not sure, not absolutely. That's why we've agreed to wait a year. I'm pretty certain, though, and it would be much better for you and me if we didn't see each other again."

"But if you change your mind, you will write?"

"Yes, but don't hope. Please don't hope."

She left.

The days that followed were days of torment and despair. The house of wishes was a shambles. It was haunted by spirits worse than ghosts, the wandering souls of departed dreams. It was as if for months I had been gazing upon a prospect fair beyond belief; then, suddenly, someone had thrown a switch and there was only a blank wall before me. I felt like Bartleby, the scrivener, for whom life was just a series of blank walls, the last of which was death.

Wounds start closing from the bottom, and so, in the

blackest moment of despair the thought came that as my blindness had played no part in our loving, neither had it played any part in Faith's rejection of me. Accepting this, I began slowly to heal.

My father's death two years before had driven the wedge of grief through my armor. When I discovered poetry the wedge became a lever, prying me open. Falling in love with Faith had completed the process. I had staked everything and lost.

16. *Chacun à sa Misère*

The habit of struggle and the impetus of routine drove me on. I strove to master the material of my courses in preparation for the battery of examinations beyond which might lie momentary success and a summer in which to recover. Examinations came, and I plodded through them.

Afterward I went out to a beach nearby, swam for long hours, and then lay exhausted in the warm sand.

Soon after this, I heard from the Director of Admissions at the Graduate School that the results of my final examinations were acceptable and I might consider myself formally admitted for graduate work for the following year. Moreover, I had been awarded a fellowship that would defray the year's entire expenses. Yale was certainly doing its best for me; the rest I would have to do for myself.

Graduate school was all Mr. Mendell had warned. Everyone else there seemed to know everything, and I nothing at all. My classmates spoke glibly of learned journals whose names I scarcely recognized, and of books I did not know. I never would have gone through the year successfully had not one of my instructors pulled me up sharply at the very beginning. After reading one of my papers, he cautioned me to review my intention of getting an M.A., suggesting perhaps the wisest thing to do was to escape quietly with my B.A. before I was discovered and dispossessed of even that.

I took this warning seriously. I set my readers to work as they had never worked before. Fortunately for me, they were all graduate students who had long since learned how to use the huge Sterling Memorial Library, and they more than earned their pittance doing my leg work. I stationed myself in one of the little cubicles in the stacks with my Braillewriter, and my readers shuttled in and out with lists of titles and notes that I copied. I went back to my room in the evening to sift and digest the day's take for the paper I was always writing for some course. I rose at five-thirty to write and rewrite, so by eight o'clock I was ready to take down the next day's mountain of material. It was a far cry from those carefree undergraduate days.

But despite all the solid months of regular labor at top speed I still had to confess Mr. Mendell had really spoken the truth. It was, in fact, impossible to hope I could cover the same ground as the others. There was just too much of it. As I approached the examinations in June, I could only hope I could make up with intensive knowledge what I lacked in extent. Since I could not cover the vast body of critical material the other students covered, I concentrated heavily on the works of literature themselves about which the criticism had been written. It was my only chance.

One day at the Lizzie shortly after exams, the instructor who had brought me up so sharply early in the year came over and sat down beside me.

"I thought you might like to know, Bob," he began, "that the committee is now sitting on the question of degrees for each candidate. I think you have been awarded yours, and though it isn't official yet, I want to be the first to congratulate you."

In the three years I had been a student at Yale, I had had everything a university can offer—stimulating contemporaries and a faculty that, like the instructor who ruthlessly laid bare my shortcomings and then later wanted to be the first to congratulate me, were as kind as they were learned. As Hamilton had fostered the development of my social confidence and had kindled my enthusiasm for literature, Yale had continued each process.

However, I had had enough training. I wanted to try to use it. I wanted to get a teaching job, to learn whether I could handle a class, to find out whether I could actually do what I had so long been training for.

The summer of 1946 was a time for anxiety and frustration. Every morning the sun rose and by nine o'clock had laid a hot, heavy blanket upon the land. Its weight lay upon my heart, and I felt like a restless sleeper under too many covers. Whatever I did, there was no escape from the heaviness and the heat.

Like the proverbial man who had given incredible care to the building of a wonderful boat in his basement, only to find he could not get it to the river, I fumed at my own impotence. How in heaven's name did people get teaching jobs? I had registered with the Yale Placement Bureau, of course, but they told me I could not depend very heavily on their services. They would do all they could, naturally; but for a college president to hire a blind instructor, well . . .

While reading the paper one evening that summer, my mother called out, "Rob! Here's something. It says they're looking for instructors. It's for the Associated Colleges of Upper New York State. The headquarters are in Albany. Here's the address."

I grabbed my typewriter, wrote an application, and mailed it that night. Could this be my chance?

After a week of suspense, a letter arrived inviting me for an interview in Albany in a few days. The time dragged by, and then I was sitting with beating heart, waiting my turn in an outer office. A voice called, "Robert Russell!"

I rose, went to the door from which the voice had called, and: "Oh! . . . I see!" said the voice. "Here's a chair. Sit down. Now . . ."

The interviewer went through all the standard questions. The last one came in the same matter-of-fact tone. "And what salary would you expect, Mr. Russell?" I gulped. I had known I would be asked this, and in a moment of bravado had determined to shoot the works.

"Twenty-two hundred," I said, trying to sound composed.

"Twenty-two hundred. I see. All right. That will be all. We have your address and you'll hear from us shortly."

And with that he showed me out. What a fool I had been! It was preposterous to ask for so much. I had priced myself out of a job! On the other hand, perhaps it wasn't enough. Maybe I had undersold myself!

Once on the train back to Binghamton, I resolved to ask for a raise if I got the job, and, if I didn't get it, I would offer myself for fifteen hundred. It wasn't until I had almost reached Binghamton that the truth dawned upon me. I had asked neither too much nor too little. Salary wasn't even a question. I didn't stand a chance for the job, but it had absolutely nothing to do with money.

As I ran over the interview in my mind, I realized the interviewer hadn't asked a single question about my blindness, about how I would handle the problems of correcting essays, having conferences with students, or preparing for my classes. Since he hadn't asked me about any of these things, he obviously wasn't even considering me for a job. When he saw I was blind, my name had automatically been crossed off his list. He had only been going through the motions of an interview.

After a week the letter came. It ran:

Dear Mr. Russell,

After much careful thought, we have decided it would be inadvisable to give your application any further consideration. Quite frankly, it is the policy of this association not to hire any physically handicapped instructors. This rejection does not represent a comment on your qualifications, which we feel are excellent. We wish you well and trust you will find the kind of employment for which you are seeking.

Yours truly,

———————

No judgment of my qualifications! They were categorically stating that no physically handicapped person could teach. They seemed to think I wouldn't mind so much as long as I knew that Milton wouldn't have been given a job there either. If I had had the same resources Milton had to fall back on, perhaps I wouldn't have minded; but since I couldn't go off and write another *Paradise Lost,* I did mind. I was furious. My God, I thought to myself, they'll be sorry someday. But when? And besides, I reflected sadly, *I'm* sorry now, and it's *I* and *now* that matter.

I hadn't quite finished swearing at the "we" who wrote the letter when another and much more welcome one arrived from George Parker, one of my old friends at Yale. George had taken a job teaching philosophy and religion at a small college in Indiana, and he suggested that if I hadn't landed anything yet, we might go out together, stopping at every college along the way to see whether they needed an English instructor. Instantly my hopes were rekindled. I would conquer the

Far West. Who wanted to potter about in those Associated places when there was the whole of Ohio and
even some of Indiana to civilize—why, except for
Cleveland and a few other places, it was still probably
unmapped country!

Though it would have been more consistent with my
idea of Ohio and Indiana if George and I had set out
in a covered wagon, we did the next best thing. We rode
gallantly forth to meet the future in Jabberwocky, a
1925 Ford convertible. On her flank sinister, a jeer and
a warning to passing motorists, was painted the immortal line of Lewis Carroll's: "Beware the Jabberwock, my
son!"

Long, hard years earlier, Jabberwocky had sported
springs and upholstery. Sitting down where the front
seat would normally be proved this. In the pile of tat-
tered raincoats and old blankets just behind and parallel
with the dashboard, a careful search would have uncov-
ered a few shreds of heavy dark material, and through
this pile rose an Appalachian range.

When George and I were securely spitted, each on his
own separate pinnacle, and when George did what only
he knew how to do, there clattered and roared before
us one of the first marketable internal-combustion en-
gines. With a mountain of luggage soaring up behind us
and a crowd of excited small boys and dogs milling about
beside on the curb, George set spurs to Jabberwocky. She
leaped forward into the road with a growl and a bark
and a sort of sneeze. As we thundered away into the brilliant sunshine of early September, the shouting and the
yapping died behind us.

"We're off!" cried George. "Shall I let her out to twenty?"

"Wait till we hit the open road," I cautioned, "and then we'll see what she can do."

For several years George had been the proud master of Jabberwocky, but her response to the controls never ceased to fill him with childlike pleasure. These controls, he had confessed to me, were really no more than means by which he conveyed suggestions. She was in an excellent mood that morning and responded with alacrity to his every whim. We were both jubilant, George and I, because we were setting out, like the pioneers of old, to meet the future. It was the beginning of his professional career and perhaps of mine.

However, I met with only a long string of, "Well, we have nothing now, but we are very glad to hear of your availability." In the vulgate, this meant *"No!"*

These stops at colleges were risky, too. Whenever Jabberwocky was willing, it was a wise thing to hang on and let her go, because you never could be certain she would start again. One night George noticed the battery wasn't charging.

"Battery's empty," he cried in despair, "and she needs distilled water." At every gas station we crept into, George would shout above the tumult of the engine, "Got any distilled water?" and then we would lurch back onto the highway.

"Guess we'll have to go on to . . ." George moaned.

"How far's that?"

"Ninety-seven miles," he sobbed.

This meant another five or six hours behind the wheel

for him. When chock-full of gas and oil and water and with the most sympathetic of men at the controls, Jabberwocky could be coaxed as high as thirty down a gentle grade, but her cruising speed lay somewhere between eighteen and twenty-one. For days we sat upon those thinly covered broken springs and did our best to while away the endless hours of flat country.

But my patience, courage, money, and posterior all gave out at once at the Indiana border. There seemed to be no point in continuing the farce of applying for jobs. This was September of 1946, and all the colleges were being flooded with returning servicemen. They were desperate for instructors, but no one would offer me a job for fear I would take it. And they were right. Then, too, if I went on much farther with George, I wouldn't have enough money to get back to Binghamton.

So George and I shook hands at a railroad station just over the Indiana border and I stood comfortably most of the way back to Binghamton.

I had hoped against hope to find a letter waiting for me from the Yale Placement Bureau, but there was no letter. There was nothing. I brought an empty heart to an empty mailbox. All the self-pity I had lavished upon myself since being driven from my Eden beneath the apple tree was abundantly justified. All that driving through the terror and confusion was to end in this! The last nail had been hammered into the lid of my coffin. I was still a white crow. I would always be white. The cool release of the Chenango rolled nearby. My pain

was private, special, unique. Isolated, alone, I had only
to be lowered into the earth.

"Ah! *Chacun à sa misère!*" cried an old French peasant
woman many years later as she passed me in the aisle of
a rickety bus in the Alps. Each to his own sorrow—and
she burst into sobs.

At first I had felt acute embarrassment and annoyance
at thinking I was the object calling forth her tears, but
then I realized they were not so much for me as for the
suffering of all mankind and her own woes.

Her voice was low and coarse, like that of one unac-
customed to much speech. It was harsh as the stony
ground in which it was rooted, a soil affording little
nourishment and even less consolation. I almost wept
with her. Great God! What misery weighed down her
soul? What had she not borne through those years of
defeat and occupation? Through bloodshed and igno-
miny, she suffered what she had to suffer; and, neither
wailing nor whimpering for sympathy, she had endured.
Her sudden outburst in that bus was neither out of pity
for me only, nor for herself only, but for every man in
his isolation. It may be that to me, earlier than to most,
this truth came home. With it came the realization that
one's only hope of preserving human dignity was to bear
what had to be borne, and in silence.

I had not endured the sorrows of that French peasant
woman, nor had she mine; our suffering united us.
"Tears are in the nature of things." *Chacun à sa misère.*

17. Launched

Empty day followed empty day. Colleges convened. Now there would be no chance even to submit an application for a whole year.

One afternoon in late September I was contemplating my melancholy prospects when the telephone rang.

"Hello, Bob," said the voice, "this is Mrs. Charles Johnson. I hope you'll excuse my curiosity, but I wondered what you are doing?"

"Why, nothing at all, Mrs. Johnson."

"I've just been talking to the Dean down here at Triple Cities College, that new extension of Syracuse University in Endicott. There seems to be some sort of muddle over one of the English instructors they've hired. He was teaching last year in Canada and has lost some of his papers or something. Anyway, he can't get across the border into the States. They need someone to take his place. Would you be interested?"

The import of what she was actually saying slowly dawned upon me.

"Interested!" I gasped, "interested! Why, yes; yes indeed . . . I would be very interested." Was it really happening?

"Well," continued Mrs. Johnson, "I'll speak to the Dean. Then you can call for an appointment. Good-by; good luck," and she was gone even before I could collect myself enough to thank her.

I took the bus the next morning for my interview. The forty-five minutes swept past almost in an instant. Before I knew it, I was talking to Mrs. Carleton Brown and Dean Bartle. The Dean asked all the right questions. They were obviously desperate. Mrs. Brown said in her gentle voice, "Would you be interested in a part-time job? That is, in teaching two instead of four sections of composition?" I screwed up my courage and made an imperious demand.

"Well, not so much—that is, not so very interested —what I mean is that I am looking for a full-time job." I sat back in my chair and waited for the effects of what seemed to me like a bombshell. It did not seem so to my two listeners, however, for Dean Bartle merely continued: "Yes, I understand that, but would you accept a part-time job for one semester? It would be a trial period for both of us, and after that, if things seem to be working out, perhaps we can think about a full-time post."

"Yes," I remarked hurriedly, "that seems sensible. When shall I start?"

"But we haven't discussed salary!" he interposed.

Good Lord! I thought. That's right. I'm giving myself away all over the place. I had better just keep quiet and confine myself to saying "yes."

In two minutes the business was settled. I said "yes" a number of times and signed the contract.

"We shall expect you in Room 57 tomorrow morning for your first class."

I actually had a job! Only a part-time one, it was true, but at the end of that first semester I would tell him I either had to have a full-time job or he could look for someone else. On the way home I recapitulated to the Dean my semester's service to the college and pointed out in no uncertain terms that he would lose a fine young instructor if he didn't cough up that full-time post. When I reached home we celebrated my success, and I went so far as to explain to my mother what I was going to tell the Dean at the end of my first semester.

"That's right," she agreed. "You tell him."

The next morning at seven, however, I was singing a different tune. In fact, I wasn't singing at all. What on earth would I say to my first class? Would they break out in open rebellion? Classes did rebel occasionally, and what did the poor instructor do?

I sat quietly at my desk while the students shuffled into Room 57. There were no immediate cries of anger or defiance, and when the bell rang, I began with halting accents to read the roll, which I had transcribed into Braille the night before. They answered the roll and, as I grew accustomed to the sound of my own voice, I began:

"Gentlemen . . . er, ladies and gentlemen. We are here for the purpose of studying English composition. This is an art of which I do not pretend to be master, but I look forward with great pleasure to studying that art with you. We are in this thing together, and I sincerely hope you will learn as much from me as I have no doubt I will learn from you." Lest this strike them as too much of a confession of my own ignorance, I continued, "Only reflect. An English teacher is like a tout at the race track who makes his money selling tips because he can't make a living betting on the horses himself. If we English teachers knew how to write really well, don't you suppose we would all be famous novelists and poets?"

This feeble sally brought a laugh, a happy sound promising well for this first class and for those to come.

At first it was impossible to tie the proper name to each voice as it was raised in our discussions. I soon realized part of my difficulty came from the students taking any seat they chose, and that I could identify them only if I made a permanent seating arrangement. The next day, therefore, I asked them to sit in alphabetical order and I called the roll slowly so each could find his proper seat. By the end of my first month I knew all my students, about sixty in number, whether they spoke to me in or out of class. This put them completely at their ease.

The permanent seating arrangement was also invaluable in helping me to solve small problems of discipline.

Whenever there was a commotion, for example, in the back right-hand corner, I knew who was causing the disturbance. Most of my students were veterans and not given to pranks, but among them were some who found it less trouble to go to college than to work for a living.

One day I heard the unmistakable chink of pennies being pitched. I knew where the noise came from, and therefore who was gambling during class time. I resented the distraction, but, even worse, I was annoyed that these students on the G.I. Bill could pitch their pennies while I had to pinch mine. I gave them fair warning, but assuming I lacked the courage of my convictions as to who the culprits were, they continued their game. The next penny that was pitched was followed immediately by the two students being pitched out, with the admonition not to return until one had lost all his money and both were content to take part in the affairs of the classroom.

The offenders apologized profusely. Nor was it difficult to detect cheating during class quizzes. Those who tried it often chose as their authority a neighbor whose knowledge was no greater than their own, but whose audacity was. Thus, when two papers were handed in bearing identically ridiculous answers, it was easy to tell there had been collaboration. In such cases I gave only one grade for the two papers, adding a note to the students that they could divide it fairly, since I could not. There were some term papers either bought from traveling salesmen from neighboring colleges or filched from an encyclopedia. The disturbing aspect of this sort of deception was that the students who did it must have had a very low estimate of my intelligence. One student, for example, did failing work all through the year but brought in a splendid term paper on Goethe that I enjoyed but did not mark. He must have thought I couldn't tell the difference between his writing and that of a scholar. I was sorry I had not made a better impression on him.

One incident that took place during the first semester gave me much pleasure. I asked a very simple question of a boy in the front row. He hemmed and hawed, cleared his throat, shuffled his feet, and asked if I would repeat the question. As I was doing this, I heard the fellow sitting next to him pick up a pencil and begin scribbling. I waited until the crinkle of paper indicated that the note with the answer had been passed and then said to the one who had written the answer, "Well, Mr. Freihoffer, since you seem to think you know the answer, perhaps you would share your wisdom with all of us." He was confused by the sudden attack and stammered he wasn't at all sure. After the class was dismissed, he came up to my desk and apologized for trying to deceive me. His apology ended with, "But what I want to know, Mr. Russell, is how you knew? I think maybe you're putting something over on us."

"Don't write so loud," I suggested.

I don't believe my students cheated any more than anyone else's. For one thing, part of the excitement of cheating was lacking. In my courses, the student didn't need special techniques or ingenious dodges. An undergraduate could just bring his notebook to the exam. I couldn't have caught him. But because I so obviously couldn't, everyone else would. Social pressure can be strong. Also, it is a relatively simple matter, I soon discovered, to ask questions for which the student must use his head rather than his book. Therefore, all my examinations developed into "open book" finals.

The mechanics of teaching soon became routine. I had gained enough confidence in myself and in my ability to control a section of thirty G.I.'s so that it never occurred to me there could be any doubt in the minds of my superiors about my competence. But they did have doubts and had set themselves the task of surreptitiously checking on me.

I had fallen into a habit of walking back and forth across the front of the classroom from the door to the window as I talked. Occasionally the door would swing open a couple of inches—by a draft, I imagined. Before I took my next turn to the window, I would take the handle of the door and firmly close it. As often as not, this would be followed by a small explosion of mirth among the students. I could not think what seemed so funny to them until years later I discovered it had been the sudden withdrawal of an administrative nose.

Student essays poured into my brief case in a never-ending stream. I took them home, where my mother read them aloud, with all the punctuation. I dictated corrections and, at the end, my comments on the whole essay. I brought the batch of corrected papers back to class, handed them out, and then arranged for conferences.

During these conferences the student read his paper aloud and we went over it carefully together. At Oxford University this is the customary practice and has been so for roughly seven hundred years. Anyone who has been forced to do this will acknowledge that there is no better test of writing.

For the daily assignments, I depended upon readers— that is, Hunnie and my mother. I took notes in Braille on all these assignments and keyed them to the page numbers in the book my students were using. It was therefore very simple to refer specifically to something in the assignment and to tell the students where they could find it. I used these notes just as any other instructor would use ink equivalents.

Since then I have found a tape recorder invaluable. Students' essays are read onto tape with punctuation. I play them back, typing my comments and suggestions, which are then stapled to the essays. Since I have my students number the paragraphs in their essays, it is very simple to refer to any specific sentence or phrase.

Also, there is now a marvelous organization, The Volunteers Service for the Blind, that will record or put into Braille any essential textbook. This invaluable service is provided without charge and our debt to them is enormous. There is, of course, still a large body of material such as recent critical study in one's special field not available in any way other than through readers. But the tape recorder, the typewriter, talking books, Braille libraries, and The Volunteers Service have gone a long way toward making the blind student and instructor independent.

I did not receive a contract for a full-time job until the spring of 1947, to take effect in the fall. I was to teach two sections of freshman composition and two sections for sophomores on the survey of literature. I had become a full-fledged member of the college community, so there was no need to recite the speech to the Dean that I had rehearsed on the bus and, later, at home.

When I was discussing my full-time duties for the coming year with the Dean, he explained that advancement in the teaching profession was contingent upon my doing further graduate work. An M.A. was really not enough if I hoped to succeed in the academic field. I knew this, but I had wanted desperately not to think about it. How could I ever get the necessary money and time to take another degree?

18. The Wheel Turns

The following autumn I shared an office with Doug Silverton, an Englishman and a graduate of Oxford. He filled me so full of stories about the place that I collected my papers and transcripts and sent them off to New York with an application for a Rhodes Scholarship. Then I forgot about it, which wasn't hard to do with two sections of literature to teach. It was a pleasant shock when I received a letter asking me to come to New York City early in December for an interview. I had miraculously passed at least the first screening. However, my happiness had a deep shadow over it—my mother did not know of my good fortune.

In spite of the months of long illness in which Hunnie

and I waited for the inevitable, neither of us were prepared for it. We could not even imagine what living
would be like without the woman whose warmth and
wisdom contributed so much to the happiness of all her
seven children. The gift of life alone—how does one
speak of repayment? To bring up a child in a home
whose center is love—who can estimate the effects of
this upon a child? Though I was twenty-two and Hunnie
twenty-four when my mother died, we both felt like little
children set adrift in a wide, wide sea.

Hunnie had taken her degree in Fine Arts from Syracuse University and was working part time designing
and advertising shoes for a small concern in Binghamton.
In addition, she read to me and took care of the small
apartment we had rented two years before, when my
mother had sold our house at 13 Edward Street. What
was left of home, it was now our job to preserve.

The hub of the family wheel had been punched out by
the mysterious power of death, and there was nothing
now to bind the converging spokes together except the
cobwebs of memory. Hunnie and I stood guard, as it
were, over the central vacancy and presided over the
cobwebs. All the others were married and were building
their own families. They had at least one eye on the
future, but Hunnie and I had only the past to remember.

There had always been something special about Hunnie. She had my mother's soft voice and the same glad
frankness. That was the crux, really: when you were
with Hunnie, you felt glad.

Ted Whiting had finished his medical training and

was then interning at one of the hospitals in town. He did what he could to help us through those first months. He would ring the doorbell and march in, dragging a fourth, and announce his intention with, "Well, I don't mind playing bridge as long as I don't have to have Bob for a partner. Bill, here, wouldn't pass his partner's opening two-bid. Come on, where are the cards?"

About midnight Ted would say, "I brought Bill not so much because he could play bridge, but because he can make such good toasted cheese sandwiches, and he won't serve them without beer. Why don't you run down to the corner and get the beer before you make the sandwiches, Bill?"

After the feast, Ted went on, "I promised Bill I'd show him a big time tonight, so he brought his ice skates. He has his car, too, so let's go. Get your skates." And off we would drive to some patch of river or to the frozen football field at the nearby park. By then all the other skaters would have left. It was like skating during the lunch hour at Hamilton, only on a larger scale. We swept along over the ice in the frosty starlight, playing tag and almost breaking our necks trying to do figure eights. At two-thirty or three, back to the apartment and the sleep that follows exhaustion.

It was during those troubled days that the letter came inviting me for an interview for a Rhodes Scholarship. I went down to New York and stayed with my friend Bob Rossiter, the wrestler and paper-cup eater, who since those days had taken his degree at Notre Dame and was then preparing to enter the insurance business.

Bob came along with me to the anteroom crowded with vital young men, each of whom was trying desperately to impress the others with his cleverness. I soon learned the interviews were running far behind schedule. People whose appointments were for eleven were only now going in, at one-thirty. I was down for two o'clock, but it would be hours yet. Rossiter and I joined in the game of "Who am I?" that was helping to amuse waiting candidates while at the same time providing them with an opportunity of frightening one another with their prodigious learning.

"My name begins with the letter B," the one who was "it" declared.

"Are you a fourteenth-century Spanish interior decorator who worked largely with taffetas?" came the first question.

"No," answered the one who was "it." "I am not Berios."

"Mmm, that will do. I was thinking of Baccagardia," lied the questioner.

"He wasn't Spanish," flashed the chap whose name began with B. "He was Italian."

"Well," joined in another, "his father was Italian—Florentine, actually—but he married Theresa of Castile and lived in Spain for the rest of his life, so I suppose you could say his children were Spanish."

I listened to this sort of thing in dismay. Einstein wouldn't have stood a chance with this crowd. I sat there on pins and needles waiting until three o'clock, when the pins and needles grew into spikes and lances. At four o'clock I was being impaled and ready to cry for mercy. At four-thirty I was called into the inner chamber.

It seemed a long, narrow room furnished with a long table surrounded by tall, straight-backed chairs. I was led to one of these by an attendant who quickly left the room. There was a shuffling of papers on the table across from me and to my right. The person shuffling the papers cleared his throat.

"How did you get here today, Mr. Russell?" he asked solemnly.

"How did I get here?" I repeated in confusion. "Why, on the subway. I took the subway from Borough Hall to Canal Street and then walked over here."

"No, no," said the voice with a touch of annoyance. "I mean, how did you get here? How did you find this building? How did you get up to this office?"

"Well," I said, still unwilling to believe he wanted to know something so simple, "I came with a friend, and we—"

"I see. That's what I wanted to know. Someone brought you here."

"No, well, not really. He's blind, too, so he didn't exactly bring me."

I suppose he thought I was either being impertinent or refusing to answer a simple question, so he changed the subject; or rather, someone else changed it for him.

"You're fond of poetry," a second voice on my left inquired.

"Yes, of course I am. Well, that is, naturally I am."

"Among the modern poets, whom do you think the greatest? Who is your favorite?" This was a ridiculous interview, I thought. I must do something. We seemed to be skittering around. I would surprise them, overwhelm them. I scraped an obscure corner of my mind.

"Hilda Doolittle. I think Hilda Doolittle is marvelous." Apparently they didn't, for there was an embarrassing silence.

"What do you feel about Hemingway?" asked a third voice, finally breaking the nervous pause.

"Hemingway!" I cried. "I don't feel really competent to express a general opinion about him. He is most certainly a superb technician in his short stories, but I have the feeling that . . . it seems to me he cultivates the hair on his forearms with great assiduity."

"You mean you think he wears a toupee on his chest?" another said. When the merriment had subsided, someone said, "Mr. Russell, there are five of us on this committee. Six of us at this table, counting yourself. How many of us have asked you questions?"

I felt as though I had suddenly tripped over a wire strung across my path. How many people had asked me questions? How could I possibly know in my tense condition? I tried to recapitulate the interview in an attempt to remember the chairs from which the questions had come and how many had come from each. The silence was electric.

"Four," I gasped. This was followed by a general stir and buzz.

"Did you ask him one?"

"No, I didn't. Yes, I did, too."

"Did you?"

"Yes, what about you?"

"No, I didn't."

"Yes, I think you did. You asked him who was his favorite modern poet."

"Oh yes, I guess I did, but what about you? Did you?"

"No, I haven't said a word. I guess you're right, Mr. Russell. Thank you; that will be all unless anyone has any more questions."

There was a general silence and I went to the door. Before I left, the spokesman said, "Will you please wait outside? We may want to speak to you again."

Bob and I waited in the anteroom until the winners were announced that evening. I didn't get the Rhodes.

We went for a beer and then out to Bob's home in Brooklyn. The next day I took my train back to Binghamton, carrying my defeat with as much good grace as I could muster.

Christmas came, and what a strange, quiet, solemn time it was. How different from those early ones at 13 Edward Street when the days were filled with the sound of crinkling, whispering tissue paper, the air heavy with the smell of cigar smoke, pine, turkey, and mince pies, and when the soft white world outside muffled the steps of friends so that the coming of each was a happy surprise. For Christmas dinner Hunnie and I went over to Bud's house. But we had to come back to the empty rooms. In 1947 we were alone, and we knew that Christmas, if it ever came again for us, must come as it had to my mother and father, through the excitement of our own children.

I went back to college after the vacation, rising again at seven to catch the bus at the corner to Endicott. I had finished my last conference and was preparing to go home one day when Doug Silverton came in, slammed his books on his desk, and said, "Say, Bob, I have been meaning to tell you—have you heard about the Rotary Foundation Fellowships? They're just beginning to offer them this year. If you hurry, you might be one of the first to get one."

"I haven't a chance unless they keep their program secret, but what do I have to do?"

"You still have all your papers from the Rhodes application, don't you?"

"Yes."

"Then I don't suppose you have to do much of anything. I belong to the Rotary Club here in Endicott, and I'll ask the club to sponsor you as a candidate, shall I?"

"Sure, please, by all means," and he did.

A couple of months later I received a letter from Rotary International headquarters in Chicago informing me I was on the short list of candidates for fellowships and suggesting that I make application to the foreign university in which I wanted to spend my year. Immediately I began writing letters to the various colleges of Oxford University, of which there are more than twenty.

I wrote to all of them—in my presumptuous ignorance even to All Souls. All Souls is not a college in the ordinary sense of the word. It has no students. Only the finest scholars are elected to it in honor of their contributions to learning. Fortunately for me, I was too ignorant to appreciate my blunder.

The answers to these applications might all have been run off from the same master sheet:

Dear Mr. Russell:

In view of the extremely overcrowded conditions of the college, we cannot foresee a vacancy for several years. You will naturally understand that our first duty is to our own students who are returning from the Armed Forces. However, if you would like to resubmit your application in 1952, we would be pleased to consider your candidacy at that time.

Yours sincerely,

One evening early in May our telephone rang. The voice at the other end was that of the Secretary of the Endicott Rotary Club. He was saying, "Bob! Hang onto your chair! Good news! Wonderful news! You're in, boy! You've got it."

I had a Rotary International Foundation Fellowship. I repeated it over and over again; the words whipped through my mind like a series of passenger trains, of which I could catch only a clear look at the last car. Gradually it came to me. I shall go to Oxford, I thought. Yes, I shall go to Oxford. My God, Hunnie, I'm going to Oxford. Me, do you hear? I'm going to Oxford. Let's call everybody up and we'll have a big party.

The evening quickly gained momentum as my two brothers, Bud and Larry, came in.

"That's wonderful, Rob," said Larry. "I knew at least one of the Russells had to have some brains. Here, let me fix you another."

"What do you mean, one of the Russells?" chimed in Bud. "I had the brains, but those textbooks at Villa Nova had such small print!"

"You never had any trouble reading the sign over a bar and grill," Larry pointed out.

"That's just it," Bud retorted; "if they had just printed those books in that size type, I wouldn't have had any trouble at all. Hey, Larry! Do you remember the time you came down and we went to Bill's—that little place with the silver chandelier . . . ?"

In the midst of these festivities, my gaiety subsided at the intrusion of two sad reflections. First, I had an eight-o'clock class the following morning and would have to think of something sensible to say. Second, would I really be going to Oxford? Considering the pile of polite refusals littering my desk, not one of the colleges had exactly sent over a delegation to welcome me.

I felt rather like Cinderella, whose fairy godmother had endowed her with everything she needed to attend the ball but who had just been told the musicians' union wouldn't let the orchestra play for more dancers than were already registered. The long and short of it was that I went to bed before the evening had well begun and fell asleep to the sound of laughter and chinking ice cubes.

While I was being refused by Oxford and getting awarded a fellowship to go there, Hunnie was having some excitement of her own. That February she met a young doctor, Tom Murphy, who had just started practicing. He was humorous, intelligent, and decisive. Tom instantly saw Hunnie's quiet glow.

Her light was all her own, coming neither from books nor social conventions but from her unself-conscious and natural delight in other people. She always brought out the best in everybody, because people knew she liked them. It was impossible to feel ill at ease in her company; you just couldn't help responding to the joy in her.

Perceiving this, Tom devoted most of his energy to courtship. His devotion extended even to reading student essays to me. He took a lively and understandable interest in the fellowship and in my going to Oxford. A few days after learning I had been awarded the fellowship, Tom was reading the letter from Rotary International confirming my award and stating the conditions on which I could accept it.

"It says very firmly," he repeated for the fourth time, "that you must be admitted to the university of your choice *before*—get that?—*before* you can accept, and *before* they will send you a check to cover your transportation."

I must be accepted *somewhere,* even if Oxford wouldn't have me. I would go to England, take a train to Oxford, and, if necessary, hammer at every door and kneel in supplication before every desk of every Tutor in Charge of Admissions. If all my efforts were unavailing, I would go on to the Sorbonne, Provence, Biarritz, or—or anywhere at all. If I couldn't get into Oxford, I didn't much care where I went.

So I stopped writing to England and started to besiege universities on the Continent. My first letter did the trick. It took me some time to realize that it had, though. The answer from the University of Zurich was in German. When I found someone who could translate it, I discovered they would have me even if nobody else would. Their letter ended with the pious hope that I spoke German—otherwise, they went on to say, I might have some difficulty with my studies. That was putting it mildly, but what did I care? I wasn't going to Zurich anyway.

I rushed to the phone and called Rotary headquarters in Chicago.

"There has been a slight change in my plans," I said off-handedly. "I am going to Zurich."

"But I thought," came the answer, "I thought you were . . ."

"Well, I was, but I've changed my mind."

"Oh, yes, I see. That will be all right. . . . We'll send you the first check to cover your traveling expenses, and lots of luck to you, Bob."

Hunnie's wedding was set for September 11, four days before I was scheduled to sail, and I was to give away the bride. All that summer we rummaged through the family relics and packed. For a year we had had a little beagle named Spot that Bud had turned over to us because he was gun-shy. Spot was the most affectionate and trusting of dogs. When the first suitcase was pulled out, it was as if we had given him a dose of some slow poison. He sat down next to the suitcase and began to whimper. The dissolution of his home had begun, but the dissolution of ours had begun long before, and Hunnie's wedding would be the final act that would destroy the symbols of our unity as a family.

First Larry, then Bud, and then Mary had broken loose from the wheel, had spun off past the rim and started their own homes, which were separate and dis-

tinct circles. Then my father died, and then Jack and
Jimmy were married. My mother's death took out the
center, and Hunnie and I were left as caretakers of the
old easy chairs, the lamps and bookcases. . . . Now Hunnie and I were turning from the past to look toward the
future, and there would be no one collection of furniture
that all of us could talk about as being "home."

There would always be a "home town" for us all, but
as strong loyalties and deep affections lose their old
anchors and find new ones, feelings about one's home
town lose their sharpness and grow vague and general.
The home town becomes a place to be sentimental about
occasionally, but is no longer a place where one thinks of
going back to live. We had presided over these old
shabby anchors, but we were now cutting our cables to
go off on our own voyages. We distributed what we
could among the others, but the old tables and lamps
would take on different meanings in their different surroundings.

While Hunnie and I were preparing for our departure, Spot's home, too, was dissolving, and he knew it.
Unlike us, his melancholy spirit seemed incapable of
hope for the future. As the days passed and the confusion grew, his whimpering also grew. Finally he howled
all day long in unrestrained misery. He was the vocal
symbol of that part of us we must leave behind. At last
we could stand no more, and, since Spot had to go anyway, we gave him to an avid hunter out in the country
who said he knew how to put courage into any dog. He
had cured lots of dogs of being gun-shy, he said.

With Spot gone, we could get on, and we had to get on, too, for September was upon us. The wedding was a kind of family contraction, the last one.

Mary came down from Portland, Maine, and Jack came east from Colorado. Larry and Bud had settled in Binghamton, so everyone was accounted for on September 11 except Jimmy, who was working in Texas and couldn't get back.

The festivities that preceded the wedding were full of frantic gaiety, ending in the solemnity of the wedding itself. Halfway through the reception Tom and Hunnie left. "You be good now, Rob, and don't forget to write," she said with a kiss. That evening Larry, Bud, Jack, Mary, and I sat around in Bud's kitchen reliving some of our family history.

"I was always the one who caught it from Dad," Larry said with a laugh.

"And you deserved it, too," Jack chimed in. "Remember the time you came home late and took off your shoes before you went up the front steps? You got all the way across that big front porch without so much as a board squeaking, and then you rang the doorbell!"

"I'll never forget Dad, either, when he opened the door. He was hopping mad when he saw it was me. He was just about to lay me out when he caught sight of the shoes in my hand and my sheepish grin. Then he started to laugh. I never annoyed the neighbors, though, the way you and Bud did. They might have heard me coming home now and then, but I never actually set out to pester them."

And so together we went back again over the old fabric of memories that had bound us all so closely together. We relived those old days until well into the morning, trying to recapture a past beyond recapturing. Then, through silent streets, we drove back to the apartment for some rest.

After a few hours of sleep, Mary started back to Maine and Jack left for Colorado. "Well," Mary said, "be good to yourself, Rob, and if you want anything, just let us know. Good-by now," and she was gone.

"You'd better be off too, Jack," I said. "I'll finish the dishes. Hey, yes; there's your cup. You might just as well take your cup along." For as far back as I could remember, we had an oversized coffee cup belonging especially to Jack. Whenever he was home it stood beside his place at the table, and when he was away it sat at the back of a top shelf in the cupboard. He had better take it with him now, I thought, for he would not be coming back. It was something of home he could take with him.

"No, never mind the cup," he said. "We'll be seeing you sometime, and let us know if you want anything."

I followed him out to the car, still holding the cup. "Just put it by the back window. It won't take up any room."

"No, I really don't want it," he insisted. "Good-by now," and he rolled slowly back out of the driveway. I couldn't understand why he wouldn't take the cup. It was especially his, and it especially meant home to him. He knew, though, that now it was just another cup, because there was no home on whose top kitchen cupboard shelf it would wait. The family home was now just a memory, and the cup would always be there in memory. There was no point in carrying around a bit of china.

Slowly I went back into the empty apartment and set the cup on the edge of the sink. It slipped off and smashed into a thousand pieces.

I myself was leaving the next day, so that night I dropped over to Bud's to say good-by.

"I saw that fellow today you gave Spot to. He was telling me he took Spot out a couple of days ago and old Spottie was hunting like a trooper. But at the first blast of the shotgun, Spot let out a howl and took off through the hills, and he hasn't seen him since."

Bill Johnson, an old Hamilton friend, had offered to drive me to New York, so the next day we rolled down along the Delaware River toward the city. It was the same journey I had made so many times in the days of the Institute. Then I used to long for a flat tire or a breakdown that would mean we would have to go back home. This trip was different. I was not miserable about leaving home because I had no home to leave.

There would be nothing to go back to again. Whatever was in store for me lay somewhere else and in the future. There was no Russell family any more—the old shell of family affection and intimate associations within which I had found protection and security was gone. The wheel had turned and turned and turned until it was no more; and, with its last revolution, Hunnie and I had been flung off.

Three: THE MIDDLE SLOPE

19. Breaking and Entering

The steamship lines will not allow the blind to travel alone, so I had arranged through Rotary International to sail with Jim Ulmer, a Texan, who also had a Rotary fellowship and was going to Cambridge. I met Jim in New York, and together we boarded the *Queen Mary*. Jim and I got on very well together and, since he was a past master at the art of introducing himself gracefully to strange women, we were seldom without the pleasure of feminine company.

When we docked at Southampton and passed the customs, I asked that my trunks be kept there until I sent for them.

"Why don't you just have them sent right up to Oxford?" Jim inquired.

"Well, the truth is, Jim, I don't know whether I'm going to Oxford. If I'm going to get in, I shall have to beat my way in. If worst comes to worst, I'm going to have to go on to Switzerland."

"That sounds like a job for a Texan. You just tell me where you want to go, boy, and I'll fix it."

"Thanks a lot, Jim, but I guess I have to do this myself."

We reached London late that evening and made our plans. Jim declared very firmly that he was going up to Cambridge by way of Oxford, where he would drop me off.

"But Oxford is out of your way, Jim. I'm sure it is."

"Listen, boy," he went on, "I've been studying the maps of the railroads here. You can't get anywhere in this country without having to go out of your way."

The next morning we took a cab to Paddington and boarded our train. It was a three-hour trip—the little engine chugging and panting along for five minutes and then resting for five minutes at some village.

"If we traveled like this in Texas," Jim declared, "it'd take you all day to get next door."

But finally we did arrive, the conductor shouting, "Ox-fo-ord, Ox-fo-o-ord!"

We left our luggage at the station and walked into the center of town, where we found a hotel, the Randolph, which, the desk clerk informed us, had been the first hotel in Europe to have an elevator installed. We went up to my room, saw it would do, and then returned to pick up my luggage. Back at the hotel, Jim inquired of the desk clerk, "That's still the same elevator, isn't it? The first one in Europe, I mean? You haven't changed it?"

"Yes, sir, the very same," he answered proudly. "Why do you ask?"

"No reason; it just sounds like the first one in Europe." And so it did.

"You're all set now," Jim said. "Is there anything I can do before I catch my train? All you've got to do is to say the word and I'll stay here until you find out where you're going. I'd like to see the colleges, and I probably won't ever have a better chance."

"Thanks, Jim. I appreciate your offer but I know you've plenty of your own business to get straight in Cambridge. I'll let you know as soon as I find out what the story is. If I go to Switzerland, you know, I won't be so far from Paris."

"You stay away from Paris, boy; I want you to get some work done. Well, I'd better be off, then. Unless I see you before, perhaps I'll run into you at Christmas in Paris."

Here I was, alone at last—a strange hotel, a strange city, a strange country. I didn't even know the English traffic laws—knowledge that is vital to anyone who can't see and who travels by himself.

I stayed in my room for the rest of the afternoon, writing letters until dinnertime, when I once more put my life in the hands of the elevator operator and his contraption. I walked to where I remembered the desk to be and asked if I could have dinner in the hotel. One of the porters showed me to a table in the dining room. My first expedition from my room was a success, I thought as I finished my meal.

I paid my bill and, feeling the comfort of growing confidence, asked to be taken to the lounge, where I sat for two hours listening attentively to the conversations around me. I could hear the waiter moving in and out with coffee. After crooking what I thought was an expressive finger and looking what I hoped was a "come here" sort of look—probably toward many of the hotel patrons—I finally caught the waiter's attention and ordered some.

Then I returned to my room, where I wrote more letters in a vain attempt to prove to myself I was doing something constructive. Going about the hotel was really no test of either my courage or tenacity. Tomorrow would be the real test. Then I would have to venture out into the strange city, find the colleges, and muster the effrontery to ask that I be admitted at this late date, just three weeks before term began.

In the morning I washed, dressed, and went down to breakfast. "Shall I go now?" I asked myself as I sipped my coffee. "No, not quite yet. I had better go back upstairs and work out my plan of attack . . . Who do you think you're kidding? That plan of so-called attack was settled for the eighth time last night; all right, let's go." Back to my room, then, where I rebrushed my teeth, retied my tie, rerubbed my shoes, and reresolved to make my expedition.

"Where would you like to go, sir?" asked the porter at the door.

"I want to go to the colleges," I replied.

"Which colleges is that, sir?"

"Why, Oxford, you know."

"Yes, sir; this is Oxford, sir."

"I know it's Oxford. I want to go to the university—Oxford University. Where is it?"

"I'm sure I don't know, sir. It's around here somewhere. If you want to go there, sir, I'd go down here to the corner, turn right—"

"Which way do you mean, to the corner?"

"You turn right at the corner, sir, and then—"

"I know I turn right *at* the corner, but which way is it *to* the corner?" This information was essential, but he didn't seem to think so.

"It's right down here, sir."

"All right; thank you very much," I said and stepped out onto the sidewalk. Down the street, up the street; which way was down? which way was up? I had no idea, but if I waited long enough to find out, I would probably lose what courage I had.

I reached a corner and nabbed a passer-by to take me across. I didn't know whether I needed to cross this street or not, but I knew I needed more help. Halfway to the other curb I began again: "I want to go to the university. Can you tell me where it is?"

"The colleges, you mean?"

"Yes, that's right."

"Well, now, let's see. They must be around here somewhere. I'm ashamed to admit it, but I don't know just exactly where they are. I've only been here eighteen years, and somehow I haven't had time to look the place over, if you know what I mean. There's a bobby; he'll know. Hello, I say, this chap wants to find the colleges."

The bobby saved the day. We were standing almost at the gates of Balliol, the very one I wanted, it suddenly occurred to me. In a few minutes I was sitting in an office and launching into my story. When I had finished, the Tutor in Charge of Admissions observed: "Yes, Mr. Russell. I think we had some correspondence with you," and he shuffled through some papers. "Yes; here we are. I explained in my letter to you that . . ."

"Excuse me," I interrupted. "I received that letter, but I couldn't reapply in 1952. My fellowship is for this year, and there isn't any other place I want to go but Oxford. I've got to get into one of the colleges."

"All right," he replied kindly. "I'll see what I can do, but there aren't any places here at Balliol. I'll try Mr. Rivers at St. Cat's for you. Meanwhile, leave me your address and I'll let you know if anything can be done. Where are you going from here? May I help you?"

"I'm just going on to the other colleges. You can reach me at the Randolph Hotel."

"I wish you good luck, but frankly, there isn't much hope."

This was the first of a long series of unhappy interviews, after each one of which my heart sank a little lower. Back at the Randolph in the evenings, I began to wonder how much German I would have to learn in order to live comfortably in Zurich for a year.

One cold, rainy, miserable morning I set off once more. I had about run through all the men's colleges and hadn't enough audacity to begin applying at the women's. At the first college I tried that morning, I was greeted by a surly clerk.

"No, Mr. Rivers isn't in. He isn't seeing anyone anyway.

"Thank you. I'll wait."

"It won't do you any good. I'm sure he won't see you even when he does come."

"Thank you. I'll wait."

"Well, please yourself," and he went back to his work.

A half hour dragged by. The outer door opened, brisk footsteps passed along the hall and up the stairs to the second floor, where a key jangled and then a door slammed. After another ten minutes the savage guardian left his letter writing and also went upstairs. A minute later he returned, grinding his teeth. "Mr. Rivers will see you," he snapped angrily and led me upstairs, muttering to himself all the way.

I introduced myself to Mr. Rivers and began my sad tale. As soon as he understood what I was leading up to, he rose from his chair and began pacing swiftly up and down his office. "Excuse me," he interrupted in extreme annoyance, "but this is really too much."

"I'm sorry, sir; I don't quite follow you."

"After all! Here I came along this morning entertaining angels all the way, and then I find you here." I accepted the imputation without a murmur. "It's just barefaced rudeness, that's all."

"I'm sorry, sir; I still don't follow you."

"Without a word of warning you jump on a boat in

New York and come three thousand miles to present yourself at my door two weeks before term opens and ask to be let in. It's blackmail. How can I say no? I would be telling you your money and time and trouble are wasted, but I think that's just what I'm going to do."

"I'm sorry, sir; I haven't made myself clear. It's rude and it's barefaced, but not quite as bad as all that. In the first place, I can go on to the University of Zurich. They've already accepted me. But, sir," I pleaded, "my field is English literature and, after all, there's only one university where one wants to study English literature. Secondly, I did not realize I had come altogether unannounced. Mr. Williams at Balliol said he would give you a call to warn you I would be coming. Perhaps he hasn't found time yet, or perhaps he's forgotten."

During my little address, Mr. Rivers' pacing gradually decreased its speed, and when I finished he was standing silently digesting what I had said. The telephone rang. "Yes, what is it?" he crackled. "Oh! Oh, yes . . . yes, he's here in my office now . . ."

When he hung up, the storm, or at least most of it, had passed. As I was leaving his office twenty minutes later, he said quite calmly: "You see how it is. You have an appointment with Professor Wilson now. He is the head of the graduate studies in the English Faculty, and he will have to approve you as a graduate student before we can even begin to do anything here. Professor Wilson will call me after your interview, and if we can proceed, I'll get in touch with you at your hotel. Perhaps we shall be seeing you again, but we must wait and see."

The door into Oxford seemed to be opening. It was only a tiny crack, but that was more than the last week had produced. I didn't bother going to the women's colleges. I put all my hopes in Mr. Rivers.

The two days that passed before my appointment with Professor Wilson I spent getting myself lost in Oxford. This is an extremely easy thing to do. I did it intentionally, so I might learn something about the place by having to find my way back to the Randolph. Except for the time I was lost in Christ Church Meadows and ended up almost having to be fished out of the Thames, it was fun.

By the appointed time, I had learned enough about the city to find my way down to Professor F. P. Wilson's rooms at Merton. Many students of literature have rejoiced in the easy grace, wit, and learning of his writing, but even the charm of his style cannot do justice to the warm humanity of the man himself. He gave me tea, and for an hour we talked about literature. He had put me so completely at ease and I had so enjoyed his conversation that it seemed only natural to ask before I left when I could come for my formal interview.

"Oh, we've already had it," he replied. "I hope you will enjoy your work here."

That evening I found a pub.

When I was summoned to Mr. Rivers' office the next day, he began by apologizing for his annoyance.

"You had good cause, sir," I said, "and though I didn't happen to be guilty of as much rudeness as you thought, I expect I would have been if I had thought it would get me into Oxford."

After we had finished the formalities of my admission, Mr. Rivers said, "Of course you realize you enter here as a commoner."

"No, I didn't realize that, but I don't mind. What's a commoner?"

"Even though you have two degrees from Yale and will be doing graduate work, as far as we are concerned you come to us legally as what I believe you call a freshman."

"And what exactly does that mean in practice?"

"It means you'll have to wear the same sort of gown as the undergraduates here."

"Fine!" I said, beaming. I would have worn sackcloth and ashes.

"And one more thing," Mr. Rivers continued. "Don't be too pleased with yourself yet. You still have to find digs. That's not impossible, but almost. The university has a list of available lodginghouses, and I'll send you along there. Here's the address. It won't do you much good, but it's a good place to begin." And with that I was ushered out.

After lunch, and in spite of the gloomy prediction of failure, I went to the address Mr. Rivers had given me. By two-thirty I was in Mr. Price's office putting my problem before him.

"An American, did you say? Well, you've come a long way. Never been to your country; like to go, though. An exciting place, I expect. Gangsters. You have gangsters, don't you?"

"Yes, yes," I admitted, "there are some, but they are

mostly out in the Midwest. There aren't any around
where I live. They're more around Chicago."

"Oh, Chicago!" he exploded. "I've heard about Chicago. Wasn't there a chap named Capone? I think you
would call him a boot legger." He pronounced "boot-
legger" with great relish and as if it were two very
separate words.

"Yes—Al Capone."

"Ah, yes! Al. That was his Christian name."

"Quite a man, he was."

"What sort of fellow?" Mr. Price asked eagerly. He
obviously wanted to hear about Capone, so I started to
tell him what little I knew.

"Oh, dear!" he finally exclaimed in great agitation.
"Did he really? Oh, I say! Here it is almost four. Have
tea yet? Of course not. Come across the street and we'll
have some in a nice quiet place and you can tell me
more."

My store of Capone legends was already exhausted but
he seemed so eager that I could not bear to disappoint
him. I manufactured them until, with a cry, he exclaimed, "Oh, they're closing! Better go back to the office.
Gracious! Five-thirty! Office'll be closed, too. Got to get
home now. My wife, you know. Did you say you were
looking for digs?"

"Yes," I said wearily, "I am."

"Just a moment," and he slipped into a public telephone booth and rang up a friend.

"All right," he said when he emerged. "Come around
tomorrow at five. I'll drive you up there. Fine place.

Good Christian place. Quite a chap, that Al—" and he was gone.

The next day when I turned up to be driven out, twenty-four hours had not been sufficient to replenish my store of tales about Al Capone. I was milked dry. Mr. Price was obviously disappointed but took it well. He drove me to a seminary where Anglican clerics were trained. They would take me in, he assured me. He implied, too, that clerical surroundings would have a salutary influence on a countryman of Capone's.

"We have central heating," announced the clergyman in charge very proudly, "but we don't turn it on until November."

"I do hope we have a nice autumn," I observed as I signed the register.

20. Going Abroad

The few days remaining to me before the opening of term I spent mostly in London going over the excellent library of Braille books at the National Institute for the Blind. One or two of the people at the N.I.B. had been to Oxford, and they gave me the names of people who had read to them and who might still be willing to read.

When I returned to Oxford, I installed myself in my little room with its cold radiator, got in touch with some readers, and embarked on my academic life. I was soon in the routine of going to lectures, having my lunch in a little café in the market, and then going to the Bodleian Library, where my readers and I had been assigned a

room to ourselves. I went back to the seminary for dinner.

It took me a month before I met the fellow next door.
John was a layman like myself, and I rejoiced to find he
didn't answer the call to chapel at six-thirty in the morning either. One evening he said, "I suppose you have to
work with readers."

"Yes."

"Do you have enough? Would you like some more?"

"I always need more readers," I said hopefully.

"Do you have any objection to women?"

"Objection? No! None at all. In fact, I prefer women
—that is, I prefer women readers."

"Well, I know a girl at Lady Margaret Hall. Let me
speak to her. I think she could probably stir up a whole
band of eager undergraduates who would love to read.
How many hours of reading a week do you still need?"

I made a swift calculation. "About twenty."

"I'll see her tonight. Pru will have you all fixed up by
next Monday, I dare say."

And, indeed, Prunella Newton did have me fixed up
by the following Monday. I spent every afternoon in my
room at the Bodleian, and every hour on the hour a new
and different charmer turned up prepared to read. Pru
organized and set up the schedule for this group my first
year, and she was followed in turn by Marion Jones, who
marshaled and goaded my readers into service for two
more years. I had four dates every afternoon, five days a
week. Yale had never been like this.

I stayed in the seminary only one term, after which I
found digs in town at 66 St. John's Road with Richard

Reason, his wife, and three young daughters. They were just setting up in the lodginghouse business, and I was their first customer. Other lodgers came and went, but I stuck to the place like the mortgage.

My fellowship was for one year only, but about half-way through that year I applied for a Fulbright Scholarship to go to Oxford, where I already was. After receiving my Fulbright, I had the bravado to ask the Fulbright Commission for another year. I never dared to inquire how it was managed, but it was; so I had three glorious years at Oxford, more than two of which I spent with the Reasons.

Dick was a great lover of bikes, and he revived in me a yearning of my childhood. I had only been on a bike twice that I could remember. The first time I fell and put the unguarded handlebar through my lip, knocking out a couple of front teeth. The second was better. After about fifty feet, I hit a jagged piece of pipe that took a small chunk out of my shoulder.

"What about a tandem?" I asked Mr. Reason one night in the kitchen over a cup of tea. "Do you know where I could get a good one cheap?"

"One of my mates at the factory has one, I think. I'll see him tomorrow and let you know."

The next Sunday he and I took a bus to a village about ten miles outside Oxford. After one precarious trial, I handed Dick's mate the money, and he and a couple of other fellows held the bike while Dick and I climbed on. They ran along with us to give us a good start and to hold us up. When their wind gave out, they abandoned us to Lady Luck and our own resources—or, rather, to

Dick's resources. His twenty-five years of cycling experience got us to Oxford, but it was sheer good fortune that got us down the High Street. If we had had to stop anywhere in those ten miles, we would have had to walk the rest of the way. We coasted in to the curb in front of 66 and tumbled off. "Quite a bike," he gasped.

"Sure is," I panted.

"Cuppa tea?"

"Thanks."

Twenty minutes later, relaxing in his kitchen and still kneading the muscles of my legs, I said, "Well, thanks for my first real bicycle ride, Dick."

"What!" he exclaimed. "You mean you never rode a bike before? If I'da known that, I'da never got on 'er with you. But I reckon you'll do from now on."

From then on, I did, and so did he. Three or four times a week we took the bike out in the evening. We covered fifteen or twenty miles through the quiet spring countryside. We stopped for a pint at little pubs, where I sat quietly in a corner savoring the broad dialect of the farmers.

Until I bought that tandem, traveling had always been boring. In a plane, train, or even in a car I never could get any sense of the country through which I was passing, but on the tandem it was different. The countryside flowed past and around me; it almost filled me. In near silence we slipped through lanes filled with the scent of clover, into tunnels of sweetness beneath the lime trees, and past the lilacs. The sudden clatter and squawking of a partridge as he flapped out of the hedge beside our

track, the lowing of distant cows, the sharp barking
of a farm dog as we glided by, the touch of the long, wet
grass or the leaves occasionally rippling across my face—
never before had sheer traveling been so lovely.

"Have you ever been to The Ben?" Dick asked one
evening.

"No. What's The Ben?"

"It's a pub out here by Weston-on-the-Green, about
ten miles out. Its proper name is The Ben Jonson."

My tourist's nose smelled a literary monument as well
as a pint of bitters, so we climbed on the tandem.

"What did Ben Jonson have to do with this pub?" I
asked Dick as we pulled into the yard.

"I don't rightly know," he confessed with some embarrassment. "Fact is, I don't know who Ben Jonson was.
Did he write something, or what?"

"Yes, he wrote some plays about three hundred and
fifty years ago."

"Do you suppose this pub is named after that chap,
then?"

"I don't know. We'll see."

We parked the tandem and walked toward the inn.

"Here we are," Dick cried with pleasure. "Here's a
bronze plate that says 'Ben Jonson, 1573-1634.' "

"That's the chap. Let's go in."

It was just like every other country pub—the fireplace,
darts game, smooth and redolent old benches, heavy oak
bar complete with dozing barmaid, and its quota of
farmers. We took our beer and sat down on a bench near
the bar. After a few minutes we drifted into desultory

conversation with our mates. I restrained myself as long as I could and then asked, "What did Ben Jonson have to do with this place?"

"Dunno," one of my neighbors answered gravely. "Uz 'e sposeda 'ave sommut to do 'ere?"

"I don't know."

"Liz, you know 'em all 'erebouts. Do you know this 'ere Jonson fella?"

Liz sighed sleepily. "I dunno." She was obviously mildly annoyed by the question. "Peoples alluz cummin' 'bout askin' such questions as that. I dunno 'oo the bloke is. Oi been 'ere fourteen year, but 'e musta bin afore moi toime."

My life wasn't all rides out to little country pubs. The program I was following for my degree required me to take several of what we would call courses the first year, after which I had to pass a battery of examinations before I could select a topic for a thesis. I had learned my lesson at Hamilton and Yale, so I began swotting away at my books as soon as I was settled.

I took a bus regularly every morning down the Woodstock Road to the center of Oxford, about a five-minute ride. I went to lectures and read until noon, when I went for lunch to a graduate club I had joined, Halifax House; then back to the library until dinnertime; then back to Halifax House for dinner, and finally back to the Reasons for more work.

I amused myself during the morning bus ride listening to the conversations around me and speculating about the speakers. I tried to sketch them in my mind. I collected people as some enthusiasts collect butterflies.

One morning the big double-decker bus groaned up to the curb. I climbed onto the platform, bought my ticket, and took a seat near the doorway. Before I was ready to listen properly, the woman next to me gave me a sharp poke in the ribs and followed it up with, "It's a strange world, isn't it?"

Aha! I thought. This would be an interesting ride.

"Yes, yes; indeed it is," I said in as encouraging a way as I could. "Very strange indeed. Makes you wonder sometimes, doesn't it?"

She considered this. "And do you know why it is, young man?"

"No," I confessed, "I've thought about it a good deal, but I can't say I know at all."

"They don't read the Bible any more; that's what it is."

For a moment my eagerness slackened. In another instant she would be wanting to know if I was saved; but it would be only a short ride, so I pushed on. "I expect you're right. In fact, I'm sure you're right. You've hit the nail right on the head."

" 'Judge not, that ye be not judged,' " she intoned darkly. "That's what the Bible says, and if people would just stop judging each other, everything would be all right."

"Exactly!" I lied without a twinge of conscience. "We meet somebody who seems odd to us, so right away we think they're crazy or something." She was wonderful, a real treasure. I would write a little sketch of her.

"That's right, young man. Just you remember what the Bible says: 'Judge not, that ye be . . .' "

"Excuse me," I interrupted, "this is my stop," and I stepped off and began walking down The Broad past Balliol and Trinity toward the library, chuckling to myself. It would be a good day; it had certainly started pleasantly enough.

Then, for some reason or other, I reached up to run my fingers through my hair, and there was my comb perched on the top of my head. I stopped, blushed, turned around, and even thought of chasing the bus to explain, but it was no use. She had made her point.

At the end of my first year, the examiners must have finished reading that same edict in the Good Book, because they let me through. The results of the qualifying exams were posted, and one of my readers told me I had passed.

"Only two failures," she said, and she read the names. Both of them were Rhodes scholars. You see, I thought to myself—perhaps I had better not say what I thought to myself. Then I remembered my woman in the bus and dowsed my evil pleasure with a pail of Christian charity.

Now that I had passed my exams, I had to settle on a thesis topic. The requirements for the Oxford B. Litt., the degree I was after, are very much like those for the American Ph.D. The main one in both cases is that you pass your qualifying exams and the orals attached thereto, and then write an acceptable thesis and pass the orals pertaining to it. The most important part of the definition of an "acceptable thesis" is that it be an original contribution of some importance to knowledge.

Under the direction of my supervisor, Lord David Cecil, I explored two or three possibilities that did not pan out. Then, one afternoon when I sat with him in his rooms at New College, he said, "How about Mary Coleridge? Do you know her?"

"No, I don't."

"She's late nineteenth century—a great-great-niece of Samuel Taylor Coleridge. She wrote one or two rather good novels, some delightful essays, and some very interesting lyrics. Go read her and see how you feel about working on her. I don't think there has been very much done at all."

"Thank you. I'll try her. She sounds like a possibility." I rose to go.

"But you mustn't expect really great poetry, now," he cautioned. "She's a minor figure, but she has always interested me. There is something special about her poetry I have always liked. Perhaps it is her personality that attracts me—I would like very much to have known her. There's something delicate, imaginative, and yet at the same time very strong about her. Anyway, you go and see what you think."

There was only one edition of her poetry. It had been collected by her friend, Sir Henry Newbolt, and published in 1907 a few months after her death. In his introduction Newbolt described her as "the tail of the comet," and after reading through the little book, I knew what he meant. There was certainly some of the fire and magic of the great Coleridge about her work, and yet her lyrics bore the special stamp of her own personality, which was only half revealed in her poems. As Walter de la Mare has said, "They were like so many doors ajar in the twilight"—doors you wanted very much to pass through to find out what kind of person lived in the house and what kind of world she inhabited.

I read everything she had published, then everything written about her, before I went back to see Lord David Cecil. When I did, he was very pleased that I wanted to work on her, and after discussing what had already been written, we agreed there was plenty of room for research on her life and her poetry. I had found my subject.

My work could not consist of reading thousands of books in the library and then tacking together different bits of each—the books hadn't been written. It would have to be in the field, so to speak. I would have to track down her branch of the Coleridge family and their friends to see what I could discover. It would be a sort of Dick Tracy operation—one suited both to my capacities and my incapacities.

One of my readers, Pamela, was especially interested in my thesis. She would come to me with great excitement, having found references to Mary Coleridge in odd, out-of-the-way places. She brought these up out of her reading like a South Sea Islander comes up puffing and blowing with a pearl, and I was the merchant who valued her finds even more than she. One late afternoon as I was leaving the library for Halifax House, she came in breathlessly.

"I've got something for you. I think I have something important—the name and address of an old friend of Mary's." Mary Coleridge had been born in 1861 and died in 1907, so it was just possible someone who knew her might still be living.

"Is she alive?"

"Yes, still alive, a great friend."

"How on earth did you—?"

"I just happened to mention it at tea with some people. I said you were working on Mary Coleridge. This funny old doctor practically jumped out of his chair. 'She was a friend of my great-aunt's.' 'Is your great-aunt still living?' I asked him. 'Very much so, and she would be delighted to think someone was interested in Mary. I'll give you her address and write to her saying she will hear from your American.' And so here you are," and she triumphantly produced a little slip of paper with the name and address. "Her name is Lady Frances—"

All the way back to 66 my head was full of "an original contribution of some importance to knowledge." Lady Frances probably held the key to my degree.

A Lady Frances sort of person would be sure to have an old trunk full of Mary's letters, and probably these would be sprinkled liberally with unpublished lyrics the likes of which would establish Mary Coleridge as one of the most significant people in the late nineteenth century. A new and complete edition of *The Poetry of Mary Elizabeth Coleridge,* with the editor's name appearing modestly in small print beneath—my name, naturally.

"You may have seen something in *The Times* about my work on Mary Coleridge," I would throw off casually to my next prospective employer, and he would wonder how a young man could be so composed about having done something that so greatly excited Lord David Cecil, C. S. Lewis, and about which even F. R. Leavis had nothing but warm praise.

When I got back to my typewriter I composed the most polite letter of inquiry I had ever written. I popped it into the mail and held my breath for five days. Finally the answer came. Lady Frances and Sir Oswald would be delighted to see me for lunch on the following Saturday at their home in London to talk about their dear friend, Mary Coleridge.

At Paddington Station the following Saturday morning I took a cab, gave the address, and leaned back to see if all this would really happen. Soon we slipped out of the main thoroughfares and were winding in and out of streets that breathed only the dignity of the past. At last we turned onto the street where my B. Litt. lived. Even the wheels of the cab seemed to sense we were rolling on hallowed ground, for they softened their whir, and the clatter of the engine died to a whisper. Not even during the blitz, one felt, had there been a sound here more indecorous than the cough of a butler. We glided to the curb, the driver softly unlatched the door on my side, gave me my change cautiously, as if to avoid the rattling of coins, and escorted me to the door.

The door opened silently and I was received by a butler who had never coughed.

"Lady Frances will see you in the drawing room, sir," he murmured and led me up the stairs.

"I hope she's well," I blurted. "She's not ill, is she?"

"No, sir, thank you. She and Sir Oswald are quite

well." I breathed a sigh of relief. We were there, and I was being ushered in.

"So delighted! So delighted!" Lady Frances said expressively. "You are the young man. Sit down; sit down. Oswald will be here presently. And did you have a good trip? Thank you, Walter. You may go."

"Thank you, madam," and Walter evaporated.

"Lady Frances," I began, my voice trembling with emotion, "you were . . . you were a friend of Mary Coleridge's?"

"Dear Mary! Dearest Mary! Those old days. Who would think that now . . . ? Those days we would all pile our things on the wagon and go to the castle. My dear mother. She was a saint. How I have prayed for her! She used to drive those beastly horses herself. I remember one night Mother got separated from the wagon. She had one of those . . . what do you call those things that give so much light? . . . a sort of . . . a sort of lantern. Yes, that's what it was. It was a lantern. Through the fields she walked all by herself. Only a lantern . . ." Lady Frances seemed to have finished.

"And was Mary with you, or were you going to see Mary, perhaps? Perhaps Mary was the one who found your mother? Did she?" I urged gently. Something curious seemed to be happening. I felt as though someone was very slowly pulling a stepladder out from under me and I was reaching for something to hold me up.

"Dear Mary! Dearest Mary! Those happy, happy days! Oswald will be here presently. We'll talk when Oswald comes. Would you like a book?"

Thank heavens, I murmured to myself. We would

talk about Mary over lunch, then. For one dreadful moment I had thought . . .

"Oswald, oh, Oswald! Here is the young man . . ."

I shook hands with Sir Oswald, and he gave me the end of his ear trumpet, down which I shouted, "How do you do?"

"Yes, indeed," he replied firmly. "It seems odd to meet a friend of . . . a friend . . . a friend . . . Frances," he shouted, "who is this young man a friend of?" Lady Frances was being spirited away by her maid to prepare for lunch and didn't hear the question.

Send me strength, O Lord, I prayed.

"Sherry, sir?" came the butler's voice from beside my ear. I jumped.

"Thank you, yes." He had come from nowhere. Over by the sideboard came the squeak and pop of a cork, the chiming of crystal, and the soft rich gurgle of mellow sherry. Then a glass materialized in my hand. I drank deeply.

"Good wine," remarked Sir Oswald, smacking his lips. "Doctor says I mustn't, but I'm ninety-three now, and if it was going to hurt me, it would have before now, eh? Who did you say you were a friend of?"

"Mary Coleridge," I shouted down the trumpet. "Mary Coleridge. Did you know—"

"Mary Coleridge? Never knew her. I expect she knows Frances, though. Frances has lots of friends."

"I bet you knew Oscar Wilde," I gambled. He chuckled merrily.

"Oh, Oscar. Yes. Quite a fellow. I remember one day he was sitting in the Royal, and I was going down the street with Alfred Douglas. Oscar got up and called out, 'Oswald! Bring that brilliant and witty young man to me.' Well, of course I did, and . . ."

It wasn't Mary Coleridge, but having resigned all hopes of learning anything about Mary, I settled for Oscar Wilde.

This was a chunk of the nineteenth century preserved for my delight. The old familiar names rolled off Sir Oswald's tongue as softly as the old sherry rippled into the crystal glasses. This setting, after all, could give me more understanding of the way in which Mary lived and the kind of people she moved among than five hundred pages on the subject. It had been a disappointment, but I had been a fool to expect so much. I was really more fortunate than I deserved.

"Luncheon is served, sir," and I was conducted into the quiet dignity of the dining room, where Lady Frances had already been installed at the table. The butler hovered about silently, seeming to be everywhere at once and yet nowhere in particular. You could be sure of his presence only by wanting something, and before you could speak he had been there, done or brought whatever you wanted, and vanished again.

When lunch was officially over—that is, when all had been cleared away except for a decanter of sunny Madeira and another of wise old port—there was a rustle of skirts by Lady Frances' chair and a maid's voice whispering encouragement and reminders.

"Oh, yes, yes; thank you, Alice. How silly of me. I had quite forgotten. Please excuse me, young man, for being so rude as to forget why you have come all this way. Of

course you want to know about Mary Coleridge. Dear
Mary." My heart leaped again. Blessed be the name of
Alice.

"I have here a precious book of Mary's. She gave it
me herself. Would you like to feel it? It is called . . .
let me see . . . it's so difficult without my glasses!" Another rustle of skirts in and out again. "Ah, yes, that's
better. It is called *The Lady on the Drawing-Room
Floor.*"

"Yes," I said hastily, "that was one of her novels and
interesting, too, but it's her poetry I am most concerned
about."

"A very precious book indeed. Have you read it, young
man?"

"Yes, Lady Frances. Thank you, I have, but it's her
poetry . . ."

"You may borrow it, young man, if you promise to
send it back. No, on second thought, perhaps you had
better not. Things do get lost, don't they? I remember
once my mother got lost with . . ."

"Excuse me, Lady Frances. Thank you. No, thank you.
I won't borrow the book. It's her poetry I'm most interested in. I even thought there might be a slight chance
of your perhaps having some letters from Mary that
might possibly have some poems in them."

"Poems! Yes, Mary did love poems. She wrote poetry
herself, you know."

"Yes, yes, I know she did. It's her poetry . . . well,
it's her letters, really . . . her old notebooks . . ."

"I have another precious book here. Henry Newbolt's

book. He collected all her poems and put them in this
book."

"I know," I said. "I have that book. I know all the
poems there. I just wondered if you . . ."

" 'Egypt's might is tumbled down, Down adown the
deeps of thought.' Beautiful!" she exclaimed, interrupting herself.

"Yes, it is," I agreed. "One of the best."

" 'Greece has fallen and Troy town.' "

"Very beautiful," I cried, "but I . . ."

" 'Glorious Rome has lost her crown, Venice' pride is
naught.' " I relaxed.

" 'But the dreams their children dreamed, Fleeting
. . . fleeting . . .' Oh, I can't remember how it goes!
Isn't that annoying! And it is so very beautiful."

I finished it for her:

> " 'Fleeting, unsubstantial, vain,
> Shadowy as the shadows seemed,
> Airy nothings, as they deemed,
> These remain.' "

"Oh, you know it, then:

> 'Fleeting, unsubstantial, vain,
> Shadowy as the shadows seemed,
> Airy nothings, as they deemed,
> These remain.'

How nice that you know that one. I will write it down
for you so you can learn it too. Oswald, have you a pencil? Give me your pencil, Oswald," she shouted.

"Mmm? What? Pencil? Certainly, my dear. Will you give Frances this pencil, young man?"

"I don't really . . ."

"She wants the pencil," he repeated testily. I passed it to her.

"I will write your name and address on this book so I will know where it is when I want it, or shall I? No, I won't. I forgot I had decided I wouldn't lend you the book because I know how things get lost. I remember once my mother . . ."

One last try for God, for country, and for my B. Litt.

"Thank you very much, Lady Frances, but what I wanted most were letters from Mary."

"Letters, why, yes. I had many wonderful letters from Mary."

"And did you keep them?" I prayed.

"Oh, dear, yes. I always keep letters. But I don't want to write any letters now. Whose pencil is this? Oswald, this is your pencil. Just put it in your pocket or you will certainly lose it. I know how easily things get lost because . . ."

"What do you mean by giving me this pencil?" Sir Oswald asked me irritably. "I didn't ask for a pencil. It was a glass of water I wanted. Take your pencil, Frances."

"Make him take it, young man. It's his pencil." I took the pencil and put it in my pocket. I had one more shot.

"Lady Frances, I have read a good deal about Mary and a family called the Nobles. They were great friends. Do you know if any of the Nobles are still alive?"

"Did he take his pencil?"

"Yes, Lady Frances. Do you know if any—"

"Oh, dear me, no. The Nobles have all passed away long ago. A shame. I expect you would have liked to meet them."

"Well," I said, rising, "you have been most kind, Lady Frances and Sir Oswald, but I'm afraid I really must be going."

"Sit down. Sit down," Lady Frances pleaded. "If you must go, we will see to that. Would you like a cab or a four-wheeler?" A four-wheeler?—and then it dawned on me that, by "cab," she had probably meant a two-wheel hansom.

"You've been most kind, really, but I shall manage quite easily."

"Walter will see to everything. I shall say good-by, young man. Oswald, say good-by."

"I've enjoyed our chat," said Sir Oswald. "Good luck to you, and tell your friend we were asking for him. Good-by, now."

Walter had seen to everything, for he had a limousine waiting at the curb for me. It was from the livery service that ferries ambassadors around London.

"Rug, sir?" asked the chauffeur.

"Please," I said promptly, to see what would happen. What felt like a tiger skin was instantly folded about me, and from somewhere far ahead the quiet purr of a powerful motor announced that we were moving. What wouldn't I have given to have swept past Jabberwocky!

"Excuse me, sir," came a voice down the plush corridor ahead of me, "the address?"

"I'm going to . . . Chelsea," I stammered.

The truth of the matter was that I was going to see my friend Ed, but somehow I didn't quite want to admit it.

Ed was a fellow Fulbright scholar from New Jersey who lived with a gusto and enthusiasm I had always envied. He vacillated between becoming a sea captain and a famous explorer, but while vacillating he was writing a thesis at the London School of Economics on "Socio and Economic Factors Influencing Decision-Making in the British Civil Service." He took this thesis, as I thought he ought to, with a grain of salt, and spent his time hunting for rare books, teaching in the night division of the University of London, and trying to keep his house in Chelsea under control and out of *The News of the World*. He had taken a large house on Markham Street and proceeded to rent rooms, mostly to women, all of whom adored him.

"I don't like normal people, Russell," he had declared to me. "Give me a dangerous neurotic every time!" and so he had filled his house with fascinating people.

"Exactly where in Chelsea, sir?" the chauffeur pressed gently.

"Markham Street—Number 30," I admitted, and put myself once more in the hands of the gods. I leaned back to enjoy my state.

It required only a little exercise of imagination to go back fifty years with Sir Oswald and Lady Frances and to be in the heart of cultivated Victorian England: dignity without ostentation, culture without pedantry, and courtesy and good taste—good taste in company, in sentiment, in food, and in wine. There was leisure, too, for reading, for traveling, for visits lasting whole weeks together, and for friendship.

The men who thronged those drawing rooms were not necessarily business associates or business competitors, not people who had to entertain one another, but simply friends who had money enough and time enough and good humor enough to enjoy one another. It was a society entirely foreign to my background. I was a twentieth-century, middle-class American, part and parcel of its views and traditions. That afternoon, though it contributed nothing factual about Mary Coleridge, gave me an insight into her world and the beginnings of a sympathy and appreciation for it I would never have had otherwise. I began to understand why we seemed a young, brash, noisy country, why people with that sort of background might not revere what we thought to be our virtues.

These mellowing reflections made me wish I hadn't been going to the American outpost on Markham Street. I felt like a spy. In good faith England had admitted me to the mysteries of a part of her culture and was conducting me in high pomp back to the border at 30 Markham Street, where I would retail my findings.

Even a spy has some decency, and I wanted to preserve what little remained to me by not openly walking across the border. The chauffeur was much too solicitous to let me off at Sloane Square so I could creep along the back streets.

The soft pulsations of the powerful engine stopped. The door opened.

"Thirty Markham Street, sir." Reluctantly I got out.

One tipped a taxi driver, but a chauffeur . . . ? I made a weak gesture toward my pocket.

"Thank you, sir; that's all right."

"Oh! Of course. Thank you very much. Good-by," and I said this last as firmly and finally as I could.

"I'll just ring the bell, sir, and make certain they are in."

"Oh, they're in, all right. They're never out. Good-by." But he had rung the bell and retreated to a position beside his chariot.

"Good-by," I repeated in a trapped voice. He was immovable in his deference.

From within the bowels of the house the clatter of dishes ceased. There was a muffled exclamation from the basement window, and then the pounding of feet up the stairs and down the hall. The door was flung open, and there was Ed. After a moment's astonished silence, he burst out: "My God, Russell, and what the hell have you got here?"

I wilted.

If chauffeurs of ambassadorial limousines chuckle, I heard this one chuckle; but since I feel certain it is not the custom among them, I must have been mistaken.

"Very good, sir," he murmured.

The door of the Rolls closed on the chauffeur, on Lady Frances and Sir Oswald, the crystal, the perfect butler, and on late Victorian England. I was back in boisterous, good-humored, middle-class America.

21. Undull Research

In the large portions of Wordsworth's poetry that nobody reads is a long work called *The Excursion*. Of all those many hundreds of lines, only one has remained with me: "Alas, I am sunk in the gloom of dull research."

It isn't a particularly good line, but it has stuck with me because it is so untrue.

About two days after my return to Oxford from Chelsea, the postman brought me a letter from a Mrs. Marjorie Madan, postmarked London. I had never heard of her. The letter ran:

> "You must excuse my writing like this, but I have heard that you are interested in Mary Coleridge, and I think I might be able to help you. If it is convenient for you to come to tea next Saturday, we can talk.

"Of course, you will want to know how I heard of you and your project. I visited Lady Frances and Sir Oswald on Saturday afternoon, apparently about half an hour after you had left. They spoke vaguely of some young man who had been inquiring about Mary Coleridge and the Nobles. Lady Frances expressed her sadness at there being none of the Nobles left. Well, I am a Noble, and I have been a friend of Lady Frances all my life, but the poor dear forgets things now. Anyway, it was lucky for you that Alice had your name and address, and this invitation is the result. Will you come?"

Would I come! Some time I must set up a monument to Alice.

I went to London and met Mrs. Marjorie Madan, a dear kind friend who was probably more responsible than any single person in England for helping to make my years there so rich and valuable an experience. She was the widow of the late Geoffrey Madan, a distinguished scholar and book collector. Mrs. Madan had ferreted out Mary's annotated Sophocles, and had copied Mary's notes for me; but what was even more important to me was her knowledge of, and sympathy with, the kind of people Mary Coleridge had known.

Mrs. Madan also opened the doors of social and literary London for me. We attended chamber music concerts, private recitals, afternoon teas, and formal dinners. I talked with actors, writers, publishers, critics, generals, lords and ladies, and comfortable country gentlemen. In their town drawing rooms, and later at their country homes, I was offered a hospitality which one seldom meets.

In none of them did I find the icy reserve and arrogance that is said to distinguish the well-to-do Englishman from the rest of mankind. On the contrary, in all Mrs. Madan's friends I found nothing but eager and sincere interest in me and my country. I did run into a good deal of frank and sometimes adverse criticism of the United States, but that was no more evidence of British snobbishness than American criticism of England is evidence of American vulgarity.

But not all the excitement of my field work came from collisions of culture. In a magazine called *The Guardian,* I found an appreciation of Mary Coleridge written by Walter de la Mare shortly after her death. His prose breathed the warmth of an admirer and a friend. Since he was then still alive, I wrote him at his home in Twickenham to ask if he could spare me an afternoon's talk. He replied, "I would be delighted. Come next Wednesday after lunch."

On the morning of the great day I went down to London to take a branch line to Richmond, where I could catch a bus for Twickenham. Many of the carriages on English local trains consist of a series of isolated compartments with no corridor. Each compartment has a large, heavy door on either side. I had ridden many times on such locals, but they had never presented any problems. There had always been other passengers in my compartment, and, when I got to my station, I simply asked which door opened onto the station platform. This time there was only one other traveler.

"Excuse me," I said, "Would you mind telling me when we get to Richmond?"

"I'm sorry," he replied, "I get off before Richmond. You won't have any trouble, though. Yours will be the second stop after mine."

"Do you happen to know which side the platform is on there?"

"Mm! Let me see. Actually, I'm afraid I don't. Still, I expect you'll be all right. Someone will tell you. Sorry, I'll have to leave you now. Here's my station. The second stop. Remember." And the big door slammed shut behind him.

The little engine coughed, and I rattled along again, alone in the compartment. A few minutes passed and we stopped. Doors banged along the train. The guard on the platform shouted the name of the station twice. Tensely I waited, hoping to hear the door of my compartment open announcing that I should have a companion.

"Bo-a-rd! Bo-a-rd!" called the guard. More doors banged, but not mine. We started with a jerk and I went on to Richmond alone.

In the two minutes that followed I played eeny-meeny with the doors. The brakes squealed and we jolted to a halt.

"Rich-mond! Rich-mond!" I picked up my brief case. Put it down. Picked it up and rose. I crossed and recrossed my compartment, listening as intently as I could. It was no use.

"Bo-a-rd! Bo-a-rd!"

I must take the chance. I crossed to the side, pulled the door handle, and stepped into nothingness.

As I fell the four feet to the tracks, I realized my danger. I landed on my feet, still holding my brief case. I tried to spin around, but my left foot was wedged. With a violent wrench I freed it and felt for the floor of my compartment. The heavy door swung back upon my shoulders, holding me against the carriage as in a pair of huge pincers. Pushing the door open with my free hand, I threw my brief case into the compartment and struggled to climb back. My fingers clawed across the smooth floor finding no purchase. With my feet I found a foothold on the wheel, and I was pushing my head and shoulders in when the door swung to again and the wheel began to turn. I couldn't move. I would have to cling here until the next station. I hoped the platform there would not be on my side.

A guard's whistle shrieked and the train stopped with a jerk that opened the pincers, flinging the door wide open.

"Hang on," came a shout. "Here comes another train!" A locomotive whistle screamed twice as the avalanche swept down along the rails. What was the clearance between those trains? If the oncoming engine or cars so much as ticked that open door, it would slam shut and slice me in two like a cleaver. Then I was in the center of the thunderclap.

When it passed, a cheery voice shouted, "Hold on a mo'. Be right there!"

The door on the other side of my compartment creaked and two strong hands gripped mine.

"Up you come, now!" With a mighty heave I was safe

inside. Leaning on the guard's arm, I hobbled out onto the platform. The door banged and my train chugged away. I had difficulty standing. I seemed to want to fall to the left.

"Are you hurt, sir?" asked the guard supporting me.

"I don't think so. I'm not sure, though. My left foot seems numb." I leaned heavily against his strong shoulder, lifted my left leg, and felt for the foot. It was there, all right.

"Oh, I see, sir. You've lost the heel of your shoe." Then I remembered the wrench that had freed me from the tracks. "I see it. It's down there. Hang on and I'll get it for you." He left me leaning against a post, jumped down, retrieved my heel, and returned, popping it into my pocket.

"Must have pulled it right off without even knowing it. Funny what we'll do sometimes. A bit shaky still, sir? Have a sit down and a cup of tea and you'll be all right."

"Thank you. I don't have time for the tea. I'm all right now. Where can I get the bus for Twickenham?"

With him I stumped the fifty yards to the bus stop and soon I was ringing Mr. de la Mare's bell.

"How do you do, Mr. Russell," he said in his deep, gentle voice. "Please come in. Let me help you with your coat. Here is a comfortable chair." And, seeing my limp, "Are you all right?"

I explained my adventure. He was horrified.

"Sit still and relax. I will get you a tot of whisky." He did, and our long, delicious afternoon began.

"It was Mary Coleridge and her friend Ella Coltman

who helped to give me my start," he explained. "They were reading manuscripts for the *Monthly Review,* a magazine that their friend Henry Newbolt had started. I had sent in an essay on some Shakespeare characters, signing just my initials, J. R."

"J. R.?" I queried.

"Yes. My name was Jack Ramal before it was changed. Mary and Ella liked my essay, and they brought it to Newbolt's attention. He published it, and that was my beginning."

The afternoon wore away, full of the sound of his warm, deep voice.

As I rose to go, he got my coat.

"Mary would be immensely flattered to think that you were interested in her, and I would like very much to know what you write about her. Will you let me see it?"

"Indeed I will, Mr. de la Mare."

"But something else," he added. "Will you write me something about sound? Our eyes make so much noise that I don't think we really hear properly. I would like to hear with your ears. Will you do that for me?"

"I will try," I said. "Good-by, sir. I cannot thank you enough for this afternoon."

"Good-by, Mr. Russell, and Godspeed." And I left.

De la Mare died soon afterward. But to read his poetry is to know that he did not need my ears.

Not only had the goddess of fortune saved me from the train, but she also sent the Cairns family my way. During an excursion in getting lost I came to a very busy intersection. Suddenly a firm hand took my arm and a woman's voice said, "All right. Now we can cross."

"Thank you. Can you tell me where the Corn Market is?"

"This is the Corn Market. We are crossing it now. Are you an American?"

"Yes."

"What are you doing here?"

"I'm a student at the university."

"Are you? Do you need readers?"

"Yes, actually I do."

She walked to the side of a building and, putting a pad on the wall for support, scribbled something and tore off the sheet.

"Here's my name and phone number. I read to people sometimes—that is, if they're reading anything interesting."

"Thank you, but—"

"Don't you want readers? Of course you do. Why don't you carry a cane? It's really very silly of you to go about without a white cane."

"I don't like to carry a white cane, and really I don't need one," I objected.

"Well, get a black one then," she advised. "Get something. Don't be silly about it. I must go now. You call me if you want me."

What she had said, she had said firmly and clearly, but there wasn't the slightest touch of sharpness or rudeness. She did seem a little odd, though, and certainly I never expected to call her.

A year later I was walking down The Broad with a gold-mounted ebony cane I had found in an antique shop. The same firm hand took my arm.

"I see you at least did get the cane. I spoke to you a while ago. Remember? Lady Cairns is my name. But why didn't you ever call me?"

What could I say? I decided to be as frank as she was.

"I thought you probably didn't mean it, and anyway, I don't expect you would like reading the sort of thing I am studying."

"Don't be silly. When people offer to do something, you jolly well take them up on it. Will you come to tea on Sunday? What is your name?"

I couldn't help smiling.

"My name is Bob Russell, and I would love to come."

"See that you do, then. No, wait! I'll make sure. Where are you living? My daughter Margaret will come and collect you. You won't be able to get out of it now, Mr. Bob Russell."

I had inquired of a friend about the Cairnses, and I was filled with awe to discover that Sir Hugh was probably England's foremost brain surgeon and a Professor of Neural Surgery at the Radcliffe Hospital in Oxford.

"But I'm going to tea there next Sunday!" I exclaimed in trepidation.

"Well, don't worry about it; some people are just lucky," my friend observed.

Margaret Cairns came at the appointed hour and took me back to the house for tea.

"Hugh, oh, Hugh," called Lady Cairns when she had

greeted me warmly. "Here is this Mr. Bob Russell who thought I wouldn't like reading to him."

The afternoon passed swiftly. One could not help being at ease with the Cairns family. As I rose to go, Lady Cairns put a hand on my arm.

"Now, just a moment. I can't read to you tomorrow because I do the washing on Monday, but I'll come on Tuesday morning at ten, shall I?"

She came, too, on her bicycle and arrived just as Mrs. Reason was beginning to do my room.

"Lady Cairns," I said, "this is Mrs. Reason. Mrs. Reason, Lady Cairns."

"Hello," said Lady Cairns, "let me help you with that bed," and she joined Mrs. Reason in doing my room. When they had finished, she said, "Now, then; what book do you want me to read?"

After two hours of solid reading, Lady Cairns said, "Please don't make me keep inviting you, Bob. Simply come when you like." She meant it, so I did.

I spent delicious weeks with them at their country house near South Stoke in Sussex, where there was always a crowd down from Oxford. After breakfast everyone went back to his room to work quietly until lunchtime. After lunch there were long walks over the downs, and then back for tea, after which Lady Cairns was always pressed by the company into reading aloud—usually from Jane Austen. In the evenings there was more of Jane Austen or music or charades.

I went down to South Stoke with them early one spring when the downs were still covered with snow.

Sir Hugh and Lady Cairns and I tramped for miles across the white silence. We found the tracks of rabbits, foxes, and deer, which we followed for hours. The still, cold air stung our faces as we followed the game across the open sweep. We were not stalking venison but hunting for a glimpse of the animals. Finally the Cairnses caught sight of a small herd of shy deer. The joys of the chase were never keener than was our pursuit on those rolling snow-covered hills and in the gently dipping valleys.

Following the timid deer was like following the spirit who had left the traces of her passage in the little lyrics Sir Henry Newbolt had collected, and in the memories of those who had known her well.

One day when Lady Cairns came to read to me, I happened to hand her the Newbolt edition. She settled herself in one of my ancient easy chairs, quickly leafed through the small book, and then exploded: "Why, Bob! Bamborough Castle! She has a poem about Bamborough."

"Yes, I know."

"Well, do you realize? I know Bamborough. We used to spend our holidays there when I was a child. The Hodgkins used to take the place, and we . . ."

At the name Hodgkin I started.

"The Hodgkins! They were great friends of Mary's! Did you know them, then?"

"Know them! My dear Bob, my sister married Robin Hodgkin, the historian, the *Italy and Her Invaders* one. I've heard Robin speak of Mary Coleridge. I think it is his Aunt Violet who was one of Mary's closest friends."

"Is she alive?" I managed.

"Of course! I think she is, anyway. She lives down in Cornwall near Falmouth. I'll write to Robin this afternoon and we shall arrange a meeting for you."

Lady Cairns wrote to her brother-in-law, who sent her by return post the address of his aunt, whose married name was Holdsworth. I wrote to Mrs. Holdsworth, asking if she could give me any information about Mary and if, by any chance, she still had any of Mary's letters. The answer was a package containing five of Mary's letters as well as one from Mrs. Holdsworth: "My trouble, Mr. Russell, is that I have too much information and twenty-five years of correspondence. How can we begin?"

Mrs. Holdsworth's letter concluded by saying we could not converse satisfactorily by mail, and that, since she would be visiting her nephew, Robin Hodgkin, in Islington in three weeks, perhaps I could come there to spend an afternoon with her. She ended by suggesting that I bring someone with me who could help us talk because she was quite deaf: ". . . and you would probably want someone to take notes."

Indeed I would. And the next day one of my reservoir of readers from Lady Margaret Hall agreed to go.

"Jane," I said later, "there's only one little hitch about this trip."

"I know there is," she laughed, "but I've taken care of that. I got my Tutor's permission to leave Oxford. She was very nice about it. Sometimes they're rather sticky, but I explained that it was all in the interest of research, and she saw her way clear."

"Oh, well, no, Jane. I didn't even know you weren't allowed to leave Oxford during term. This is another hitch. Have you ever ridden a tandem?"

"No," said Jane, "I never have. Why?"

"Because Islington is the place we want to go, but British Railways have never heard of it, so we shall have to take the tandem with us on the train to Camden and bike the three miles from there."

"I never have," she repeated, "but I expect I could. We'll try it, shall we?"

Jane was so innocent and sweet that I hated to do this to her, but the tandem was the only way we could be sure of getting there and back. Back! There wasn't any train back from Camden that day, so we would have to go the seven miles to Morton-in-the-Marsh in order to catch a return train to Oxford.

I had the tandem greased and all ready to go on the morning of the great day, and I also had a couple of stalwarts on hand to hold the bike while Jane and I clambered on—it was a boy's bike front and back. Jane laughed as she climbed on. The stalwarts shoved us off, and we went careening down St. John's Road in the hope of reaching the Oxford station in one piece, or, rather, in three pieces, counting the bike. Though I was an old hand at tandem riding by this time, my experience was all on the back seat, and however skilled the chap in back is, he can't compensate for an error in judgment of the fellow in front when it comes to turning corners. We scraped a few lampposts, frightened a couple of dogs, and scattered a few clumps of chatting pedestrians. But we got to within two blocks of the station without having to stop—then we were stopped by a red light. We picked ourselves up and brushed ourselves off.

"Since we're so close," I suggested, "let's walk the rest of the way, shall we?"

"Good idea," Jane gasped.

We put the bike on the baggage car and chugged to Camden in comparative comfort.

"What we have to do," I said after the little train had panted along for an hour and a half, "is to make certain of the directions to Islington before we start off, so we don't have to start again."

"That's right," Jane agreed heartily. "We have to know the way backwards."

"Jane," I confessed, "we don't really have to know it backwards. We have to come back a different way—by Morton-in-the-Marsh, you know."

"Oh!" she observed, and then, with a pause, "I didn't know. Is that farther?"

"I'm not really certain," I hesitated, "but the thing to do is to make sure about the way from Camden."

We were given specific directions by the stationmaster at Camden. Both of us knew exactly where to turn, though Jane had to do all the turning. When we felt as confident as we thought we were ever going to feel, we leaned the tandem against the side of a luggage cart, climbed on, and induced the porter to give us a push. We were off again. This time it wasn't through the grueling traffic of Oxford, but along peaceful country roads, and the three miles with all their turns slipped gently by.

"You're doing very well, Jane," I commended. "You'll be an old hand by tonight."

"It's not so bad once you get used to the steering," she said, "but are you pedaling?"

"Jane!" I cried. "What a thing to suggest! Of course I am!"

"That's good! Oops! There's the white house, so this one must be it."

We turned off the road and skidded to a halt without either of us falling over. We were improving.

The door swung open.

"Hello," said an incredulous voice. "You did get here, then? When we heard you were coming by tandem . . . I'm Mrs. Hodgkin and you must be the Robert Russell who is so interested in Mary Coleridge."

"How do you do, Mrs. Hodgkin. This is Jane Creed, and with Jane's steering, Mrs. Hodgkin, I believe we could get to Australia."

"We could if he would pedal!" Jane laughed.

"Do come in," said Mrs. Hodgkin kindly. "Mrs. Holdsworth is very eager to see you both."

And Mrs. Holdsworth was wonderful. Though well along in her eighties, she swept away fifty years as if they had been a day and talked of Mary and Mary's poetry as if she had only just come from a visit with the Coleridges in Cromwell Place.

She described how secretive and shy Mary had been about her poetry, how Mary had finally filled a little notebook with poems for her alone when she had been Violet Hodgkin. It was a tiny white book with *Verses by Vespertillio* on the first page. Violet, in her own words, "betrayed Mary's trust" and put them into the hands of Robert Bridges, who had just married one of her cousins. Mr. Bridges, the great poet and scholar, read them with the excitement of discovery. Violet explained to Bridges that she had put them where he would find them but that she could not reveal who wrote them without the author's permission. Then there was the terrible confession to Mary. "Naturally, Mary was really *thrilled,* overjoyed to think that Mr. Bridges liked them," and so she had brought Mary and Robert Bridges together.

Then Mrs. Holdsworth produced those letters from Mary in which she described her first visit with Bridges and his criticism of what he had read. Riches and jewels were being tumbled into my lap from an inexhaustible chest. Mrs. Holdsworth was reliving all those days of fifty years before and documenting her memory by producing long and fascinating letters from Mary. I was listening in rapt attention, and Jane was writing furiously. Suddenly Mrs. Hodgkin broke in: "You must excuse me, but it's ten to six, and if you are going to catch your train at Morton-in-the-Marsh, I think you had best get ready."

"But you will treat these with care, won't you?" pleaded Mrs. Holdsworth. Treat what with care? I wondered. Then I realized she meant the letters. She was letting me take her beloved letters.

"I will guard them with my life," I said slowly, so she could read my lips.

"Good," she replied. "There are more, Robert; many, many more. Twenty years of them." My head swam. "But I could not bring them all. You must come to see me in Cornwall, perhaps after the New Year, will you?"

"I would be glad to walk all the way."

"And will you bring your enchantress with you?"

"I would love to come," said Jane, "but my plans for the Christmas vac are all set. I'm afraid I couldn't get away, but I'm sure Bob and I can find someone who would be delighted to help."

Our good-by's were hurried because Mrs. Hodgkin was ushering us out the door to make sure we caught our train.

"You just go up that hill there. It's very steep, but once you get to the top, it's downhill most of the way."

We walked the bike out into the evening mist and to the top of the hill, which was very steep indeed. Once at the top, we propped ourselves up by the hedge, climbed on, and gave a push that sent us across the road and into the ditch on the other side. Jane was magnificent. Instead of panicking, she rode out the crisis and steered us slowly back onto the road. We were off. Quickly we gathered speed, and soon we were hurtling along with the tires singing on the wet pavement.

"Pretty misty," said Jane. "Can't see a great deal, really." Pause. "Suppose we met a car?"

I thought this over carefully for a few moments. "Well, suppose we didn't?" I countered.

And we didn't.

Twenty minutes later we rolled into what turned out to be Morton-in-the-Marsh. Two hours later we left the train in Oxford, took the tandem off the baggage car, wheeled it out of the station, climbed up, and rode off like a couple of professionals.

The next time Jane turned up to read at the library,

she asked if I knew that Elisabeth Shaw, one of my other readers, lived in Cornwall near Falmouth.

"Does she?" I exclaimed. "I didn't know that. That's very interesting. Do you think she would be willing to do the reading of the correspondence at Mrs. Holdsworth's?"

"We could ask her," Jane replied.

"Part of the trouble, Jane, is that I probably ought to stay with whoever is going to do the reading, so what this amounts to is asking Elisabeth to invite me for a visit."

"Maybe she would," said Jane. "She's my best friend, and I think I could explain to her. Why don't you come to tea with us on Friday, and the three of us will talk it over?"

That sounded good, very good.

Elisabeth had been reading to me for some time. She was studying for her degree in English, and she had begun to interest me long before I knew she lived in Cornwall. She had a musical laugh and a rich velvet voice. To listen to her reading poetry was to hear the poet's emotions blown through bronze or breathed through silver.

Quite often when she came to the library, I set aside what I had been reading and gave her some W. H. Auden or perhaps E. E. Cummings. She knew only a little Cummings, so I had the pleasure of introducing her properly. She realized that I liked listening to her, so she began to bring her own books. We took some Sunday afternoons for poetry, too. The sound of her voice started to intrude on my thoughts at the oddest moments.

While bidding a small slam after dinner at Halifax House, I seemed to hear her reading a Rilke Elegy, and before I fell asleep, her warm sparkle opened an unexpected door and came to me down the corridor of a memory.

22. A Better Fate

Christmas came and went. I put the tandem on the train for Truro and a couple of days later boarded the Cornish Riviera at Paddington.

Elisabeth's mother had been widowed ten years earlier, and she had brought up her family of five children on courage and a shoestring in a rambling old cottage in Tresillian, a little village in the heart of Cornwall.

Robert, the eldest, had made his way through the Royal Academy of Dramatic Art on scholarships, and he was then with the Stratford Shakespeare Company. Elisabeth had won a State Scholarship to Oxford, while Joanna, her younger sister, had won a scholarship to Cambridge. Sandy had a scholarship to Epsom College, one of

England's "public schools"; and Wendy, the youngest, had her scholarship at Christ's Hospital, a famous old school near London.

When I arrived, Mrs. Shaw was getting ready to go back to college herself. Now that her children were all away at school, she had decided to train as a teacher, so she was going to the government teachers' training college at Cheltenham. Elisabeth was doing the housekeeping because her mother was busy writing the essays she should have written at the beginning of vacation. Her warmth filled the house, from the oven where she made pasties to the sofa where she sat with ten-year-old Wendy teaching her to draw. As I sat nearby, the rhythms of Rilke and Cummings were gradually drowned out by the tom-tom of my pulse. I was beginning to live what they only talked about.

In the next two weeks, Elisabeth and I took long walks by the little Tresillian River, and as we sat on the bank, the gulls and curlews wheeling and calling far above us, a quiet stole over us both. Though it was the first week in January, the hazel catkins were out, there were newborn lambs in the fields along the lanes, and the daffodils growing wild in that strange and wonderful place were just coming up. Spring was beginning in Cornwall; and, in that spring along the river, we could feel the presence of love.

Elisabeth's shyness gradually dissolved, and as she tried to describe her beloved Cornwall, I began to understand that the swans on the glassy ponds, the sloe blossom delicate as frost in winter along the towpath, the beech trees with fresh young leaves high above us, the gray lichen on the oaks by the water's edge, and, above all, the river—its satiny mud flats at low tide and its great peace at the full—all this had been a part of her growing, as the Chenango had been a part of mine. We understood each other. She picked primroses and showed them to me, and our fingers trembled when they touched.

And it grew, and it grew, and it grew—coming over us like an English spring.

Nobody knows when spring comes to England. It starts somewhere back in early February, or even January or December in Cornwall, and slips up the island under cover of the valleys and thickets. It steals up hillsides and sneaks out of hedges to primrose the woods. One can always tell it is there, that it's all around, but it's hard to know exactly where it is until it is over. It is gentle and elusive. That is why there is such great excitement in England over the first cuckoo—he tells you that the coming is over and spring is here.

That time with Elisabeth in Cornwall were the days just before the cuckoo. The secret was all around us and yet nowhere in particular. It had been creeping up for more than a year, stepping lightly on the poetry of Rilke, slipping on through the edges of a laugh, gathering slowly in the atmosphere of the college gardens where we had seen Shakespeare's *Tempest* six months before.

Now it gathered momentum and power.

By the time we went to see Mrs. Holdsworth, Elisabeth was saying things like, "Do you think she will let *us* see all the letters?"

"We'll ask her, shall we?"

Mrs. Holdsworth quickly sensed a romance in the making, and she talked about "you two young people" in a special sort of way. "I think Mary would have liked you both."

She produced treasure upon treasure, including two little notebooks in Mary's own handwriting, with many unpublished poems in them.

"And here, too," she said, "is the little volume I laid on the hall table in the Bridges home where Mr. Bridges would be sure to find it. Then, here are the notebooks in which Mary copied out most of her poems for Mr. Bridges. Do you see? Her poem is on the right-hand page and all this on the other side is what Mr. Bridges wrote about it—his criticism. There are two books of this."

We had struck gold. In these pages one could trace the growth of Mary's poetic powers as they were developed under the guiding hand of Robert Bridges.

"But you two would like to walk in the garden before tea. Come back in twenty minutes." She knew, perhaps, more than we did ourselves.

When we returned, she was rested.

"Do you see? When you are old like me, you will need rest, and while you are young you need love. Don't blush, my dear, it's very true, and you are very beautiful. You are beautiful and young, so do not waste the time you can spend together. There may come a time when you cannot be together, and then you may be old and alone and need rest."

"May I take these books with me?" I ventured to ask before we left. She hesitated.

"I think . . ."

"Oh, please," Elisabeth pleaded.

"All right, my dears. Take them; take them quickly before I change my mind, and God bless you both."

We took our treasures back to Tresillian. Greater treasures still were the river, the catkins, the curlews, and the daffodils.

> wholly to be a fool
> while Spring is in the world
>
> my blood approves,
> and kisses are a better fate
> than wisdom
> lady i swear by all flowers.

If we were to be married, we had to have a place to live.

Housing wasn't easy to find. I thought of my Mr. Price, but I couldn't contrive any more stories about Al Capone, and even if I could have, he might have tried to put me back in a seminary. We watched the papers and finally saw an advertisement for a cottage about twenty miles from Oxford.

"That's what I need," I said. "A good quiet place to finish writing the thesis."

"Let's go and see it."

Childrey was a hamlet three miles from a bus line. After leaving the bus, we walked along the bridle path over the chalk downs from Wantage, then down into the village itself, complete with elm trees, duckpond, and swallows. Then along a lane between paddocks where sleek race horses grazed and then at last through an old swinging gate into a spacious garden breathing of roses and Easter lilies and verbena. Down the lavender-bordered walk to a lovely old Elizabethan cottage. The Close was like Ann Hathaway's cottage—white plaster streaked by ancient black timbers, and a high-peaked yellow thatched roof.

Inside it was cool, like an old stone farmhouse, and its two kitchens were farmhouse kitchens with red flagstone floors. In the massive oak beams were old hooks from which once hung sides of bacon and big brown hams, and everywhere was the smell and the shine of oak that had been polished for five hundred years.

The two ladies who owned The Close wanted to rent half while they lived in the other half. The half to be rented contained two kitchens, a sitting room with Tudor roses set in the plaster of an enormous fireplace, two bedrooms, one of which listed sharply to starboard, and a bathroom. We climbed to these bedrooms up narrow stairs that rose as steeply as a ship's ladder. All about the house were hawthorn thickets and fields where stable owners grazed their thoroughbreds.

How could we refuse it?

To be married to Elisabeth in the spring on the Berkshire downs with the larks going mad with joy and our own thatched cottage and a rose garden and the rolling downs—we had worlds to discover and explore together, and every one more wonderful than the other.

Toward the end of April, I came back to earth with a terrible shock.

"Darling," I moaned, "there's the thesis. I've got to finish, or, rather, *do* the thesis."

"It's almost finished, isn't it? I mean, you only have to rewrite a little? When is the deadline?"

"The fifteenth of June, twelve noon on the fifteenth. And it's more than just a little rewriting. There are yards and yards that haven't really been roughed out properly yet."

"What have you been doing all this time?" It was a legitimate question, but coming from one's new bride, it seemed unfair.

"I've been marrying you, for one thing."

"We've got to set to work, then."

We did set to work. Each morning I labored and struggled, trying to organize into coherent groups the wealth of material I had gathered. In the afternoons I wrote the parts I had organized in the morning, and in the evenings I transferred what I had just done into typing. I went along like this, putting in a ten-hour day, for about three weeks. Then finally I said, "All right; the rough draft is finished. Now we'll have to type out fair copies and revise as we go along." This sounded good— rather professional, I thought—and would probably take us about a week. I had made inquiries at a bookbinder's in Wantage, and he said that if I got the manuscript to him on a Monday, he could have it finished by the following Thursday. I could take it to him, then, on June eleventh, pick it up on the fourteenth, and wander carelessly into Oxford on the fifteenth to turn it in. June eleventh was about two weeks off—surely time enough in which to retype and do the small bits of revision that would probably be necessary. I could relax.

However, after the first hour it became very apparent that what I had airily thought of as slight revisions amounted in fact to complete rewriting. Passage after passage, page after page had to be roughed out, typed again, gone through, and then typed in finished form. Elisabeth was heartless.

This is the sort of thing we disputed about: Mary Coleridge died in 1907 at the age of forty-six after an appendicitis operation. It had only recently been learned that this was an illness that might be cured by surgery. In Mary's case, however, the operation was unsuccessful. I had written:

"It would be nice to be able to say that, had she but lived, the roster of immortal English poets would have included the name of Mary Elizabeth Coleridge. However, her genius was nipped in the bud. I would *like* to be able to say this, but, after all, she lived to be forty-six."

"That's no good!" Elisabeth stated firmly.

"It's not *meant* to be *good*," I complained. "It's a sort of little joke, you know."

"It's not terribly funny."

"No, it's not meant to be terribly funny. Examiners aren't the sort of people who like terribly funny jokes. They like this sort, though—a mild kind of joke—a little lame, but sort of funny. That's what they like, really."

"How do you know that's the sort of joke they like?"

"I just know. Anyway, I used to be an examiner.

That's the kind of joke I like. It's my favorite sort. You are too young to understand how it is with examiners."

"If you think I'm that young, why did you marry me?"

"I thought I could educate you properly."

"I'm going to bed. Good night. Please attend to the sitting-room fire when you're finished here."

"Now wait. I'm sorry. I didn't mean that."

"Well . . ."

"It's not a very funny joke. I agree. It's a lousy joke, really. We'll cross it out, shall we?"

Revising was a hard job.

We had two solid weeks of it. We averaged about two hours of sleep a night or maybe an afternoon. Whenever we gave out, we lay down and slept, after having set our alarm to go off a couple of hours later. We would work all through the night and on into dawn.

We took ten-minute breaks when the birds began their chorus. We flung open the sitting-room window and leaned out into the cool, damp freshness and listened to the morning song. The robins usually started with some nervous twittering. Then a blackbird would let go his long, sweet, clear whistle. The thrushes joined in, as if they were afraid of being left behind, and did their best to make up for lost time. Then up from the downs went the first lark like a rocket of joy, and the chorus was in full career. Late and lazy and not at all certain of his proper interval, the cuckoo made his entrance. I had never known that a cuckoo was capable of anything but his two familiar notes, but very early in the morning he slips and slides around for three or four minutes before he finds his interval. Those were dawns we shall always remember.

I typed the last footnote about six o'clock on the morning of June eleventh. We packed the three copies separately, put them in the paniers of the tandem, and rode up over the bridle path to Wantage. We handed them to the binder, got back on the tandem, and struggled home, where we slept for twenty-four hours.

"Isn't it glorious!" I cried as I woke. "We've finished, and on schedule, too."

"It's not over yet," Elisabeth cautioned. "We have to read through it, you know, and then there are the orals. When are you supposed to go for those?"

"July fifth." The examiners had very kindly given me an early date for my oral examination because we had booked passage for the States on July eighteenth.

"How is the cider supply?"

There was a little niche in one of our kitchens obviously intended as a place to set up a barrel. When I first discovered this niche, I ordered a barrel of cider and set it up there. Every now and then the cider men would turn up in their truck, take away the empty keg, and put in a new one. We hadn't drunk any cider for the past two weeks because we had been too busy, for one thing, and, as I discovered, we were out of it. I immediately ordered another keg.

Tuesday, the twelfth, passed, and Wednesday came, but still no cider. Wednesday afternoon I called the brewery, and they said they would certainly deliver it the following day.

"Good. We shall have cider while we go over the thesis."

Thursday morning we rode into Wantage and picked it up. Three good, solid "original contributions of some importance to knowledge" they were, I hoped rather desperately. Elisabeth put them in the paniers and we started back across the downs.

"Can't you pedal a little harder?" asked Elisabeth.

"I'm trying," I said, "but actually I don't feel that spry, somehow."

"Oh, you're just hungry. You'll feel better after lunch."

I didn't, though. I couldn't eat any lunch, and I didn't feel better at all.

"Just nerves. Lie down for a while, and I'll go through the first chapter by myself."

A couple of hours later Elisabeth called to me. "I say, the cider's here!"

"Tell them to go away," I moaned.

"What? What's the matter?" and she came running up the stairs.

"I'm going to die!" I breathed.

"Stop it, now. What's the matter, darling? Do you really feel ill?"

"It's my stomach! I'm going to die, die just like Mary. It's appendicitis for sure. Had I not been nipped in the bud . . ."

She disappeared and returned after a few minutes. "The doctor will be here soon."

"He'll come too late, I know."

About two hours later the doctor meandered over

from the other side of the village. After a quick examination he said, "Have you a telephone?"

"Yes, downstairs."

"I'll be back in a minute."

I could hear his voice. "Give me Oxford, please; the Radcliffe Hospital. Hello, Radcliffe? This is Dr. Brooks at The Close, Childrey, about three miles from Wantage. Can you send an ambulance right away? I've got a rather hot case of appendicitis here."

"I told you so!" I cried. "You see? You'll be sorry for all those mean things you said about my jokes."

"Oh, darling . . . But what about the thesis!" Elisabeth almost wept. "What shall we do about the thesis?"

"Never mind the thesis. You're about to lose your loving husband. When I promised to 'honor you with my body,' I didn't mean it in just this way. . . . Put the thesis in the ambulance with me. If I live, I'll send one of the nurses over with it in the morning. If I don't, lay it at my head."

"I'll go with you. That will save the bus fare. Won't it? Good idea, really. I'll go in and find a room somewhere. I'll correct the copies tonight and take it in myself tomorrow morning."

How could one's bride be quite so levelheaded! It was almost indecent.

"Bus fare!" I groaned bitterly.

After two more hours of misery, the ambulance rolled slowly up to The Close and I was carried out on a stretcher, with Elisabeth marching along beside me carrying the three copies of the thesis.

"May I ride in the back with him?" she asked.

"Please yourself, miss," drawled the middle-aged nurse.

"I'm not Miss, I'm Mrs.," Elisabeth said hotly.

"Suit yourself, miss," observed the nurse absently, and she began to hum quietly to herself. Elisabeth climbed into the back with me and the nurse, and the ambulance crept along the road toward Oxford. After about fifteen minutes I unground my teeth and snarled, "Can't they go any faster?"

"I s'pose they could," observed the nurse, lapsing again into her quaint little hum.

"For God's sake, tell them to hurry, will you?"

"Now, don't you get upset. Everything'll be all right, I expect. We did 'ave a fast trip th'uther week, though. Did everything we could. Garge had the pedal right down to the floor practically the 'ole way. Didn't do no good, though. Chap 'ad a bad 'pendix. It bust on the way. Think 'e's still on the critical list. Funny thing about them 'pendixes. Just can't tell about 'em."

While the nurse was easing my pain with these restful reflections, I could hear the driver and his helper chatting away in front.

"Got any 'bacca, Garge?"

"Yep; just a minute," and the ambulance slowed down and swung toward the curb.

"Oh, don't bother to stop. I'll git it. Is it in this pocket?"

"Yep; can ya manage?"

"Fine." Pause. "What da ya think o' this dry spell,

Garge? If we don't get a bitta rain soon, my broadbeans are just gonna curl up and die."

"I seed a rabbit in the garden th'uther night," Garge replied, "and 'e sniffed round, but that lettuce was so dry he jis turned up 'is nose."

"Elisabeth! Tell them to hurry!" Elisabeth leaned forward and tapped Garge on the shoulder.

"Hey, hurry up, can't you? This is an emergency." Garge increased the pressure on the accelerator slightly.

"Doin' what us can, miss. No, that rabbit woulden touch it."

" 'Ere's a bad un, now," remarked the nurse. "Picked up three fellas at this 'ere corner last week—'ad a wreck, they did. What a mess they was. Not one of 'em . . ."

"Oh, God!" I growled in desperation.

"Ah, 'e's a bit edgy, ent 'e? Poor chap! Well, like I sez, there uz these three chaps . . ."

At last we rolled up to the hospital and I was carried in, with Elisabeth still marching alongside bearing the three copies. I was deposited on an examination table, where I seemed forgotten by everyone except Elisabeth, who was just beginning Chapter Two.

"You don't press hard enough on the typewriter on whatever it is you're supposed to press on for the capitals," she remarked as she worked away with her pen correcting the errors. *"Interrupt* has two *r's."*

"Hello, what do we have here?" asked a sleepy voice, and hands began to push and prod me.

"King Edward's complaint," I moaned.

"Delirious, eh?" muttered my tormentor.

"I'm not delirious at all. Don't you know that appendicitis went unsung until King Edward got . . . they operated on her, too, but it was no use."

"Oh, you think you have an appendicitis, do you?"

"Of course I have. Get me to the operating room. I want to warn you, though, that you'll have to wait for your money until I'm famous, and right now that seems very unlikely."

"I'm not worried about my money," the intern replied. "I'm from Bucknell, and anyway this is National Health. You look like a wrestler to me. I used to do a little wrestling at Bucknell."

"Did you!" I said, brightening. "Did you ever run across a fellow named Carl German? I think he was from around there. He wrestled 145 for—ouch—Columbia."

"German? Yes, I think he was at Wyoming Seminary before Columbia, wasn't he?"

"Yes," I cried excitedly. "You knew him, then? I met him when I was wrestling in high school. He was a mean man on a switch—had a perfect switch! . . . I remember . . ."

"We'll talk about that later. I think we'd better get you into the operating room. I'm going to give you a little needle. It won't hurt." And he drove a great dock spike into my arm. "There. You see, it . . . 'asn't ba' . . . 's' . . . ." Already his voice had faded away

As the fog bank over my mind began to dissolve, heaving around in patches and tatters, down one clear channel of consciousness came the question in a sweet female voice: "Wha's a 'esi'?"

"Mmm? Speag a liddle 'ouder."

"What—is—a thesis?"

"It's part of the human heart. Are you a nurse? You're a nurse, aren't you?"

"Yes," and she laughed, "but no one ever said anything about . . ."

"Then you have a great deal to be thankful for. Why do you want to know?"

"On the operating table and ever since they brought you in here, that's all you've been talking about. You kept asking if the thesis was in. In where, anyway?"

"It's just something that's been on my mind." The patches of fog spread again and closed out the voice. . . .

"Hello, do you feel better now? Would you like some lunch?"

"Mmm?"

"Your wife just called and left a message to say everything is all right. She got the thesis, whatever that is, in at twelve this noon."

Once back at The Close, we had to think seriously about packing our worldly possessions. I did most of the thinking, and Elisabeth did most of the packing. Braille books are extremely cheap in England. A Shakespeare play, for example, which would cost about $3.50 in the States, could be bought there for forty cents. I stocked up. I had also bought all the poetry I could afford, so Elisabeth had about two hundred volumes to pack.

Braille volumes are big, about twelve by fourteen by

two inches, and a book like *The Oxford Book of English Verse,* which in the print edition one can stuff into one's coat pocket without much trouble, in Braille runs to ten volumes, or about three armfuls. Elisabeth struggled away night and day, wrestling with those huge packages. A kind neighbor who saw her staggering back and forth across the fields to the little post office with the parcels took pity on her and lent her a wheelbarrow.

When all was packed, we left that beautiful place with heavy hearts and with promises to ourselves that some day we would come back to the larks going mad in May, and the blackbirds whistling in the hedgerows, and where the cuckoo announced our spring.

Back in Oxford, we had scarcely time to get settled with our friends the Reasons, when I had to go for my orals.

Such examinations are sore trials under the happiest of circumstances, but in my state of exhaustion and weakness they were two hours of torture. When they were over, I wandered back to 66 in a daze, stretched out on the bed, and fell asleep instantly. Elisabeth had gone off to say good-by to some of her friends, and when she returned she woke me.

"How did it go, darling? Do you think it went all right?"

"They picked it full of holes, and there were places where they didn't have to do much picking. It's no go— no degree, I mean."

"Oh, dear! That's terrible, isn't it? Still, you can say you studied at Oxford, as if you couldn't be bothered about anything so pedestrian as a degree. It will sound rather good, don't you think? You got some education instead of a degree."

"It's the deans and heads of departments I'm thinking about."

"Well, don't. If some of them won't give you a job, somebody else will. Cheer up. Mrs. Reason has put a kettle on for us. We'll have some tea and then you'll feel better."

Elisabeth ran out to get the kettle. I was asleep again before she returned. Then she was shaking me gently. "Bob! Bob! Wake up, darling. It's all right. One of the examiners just biked over to say the thesis is all right. You have your degree. She said lots of lovely things about it, and we're invited for sherry tomorrow."

We had a quiet celebration with the Reasons that evening at The Trout, a beautiful little sixteenth-century inn on the river just outside Oxford.

"You and Elisabeth should have a son," Dick said.

"I hope so, someday," said Elisabeth dreamily.

"If and when we do, Dick, I'll name him after you," I said.

"Richard Russell," he said, and he savored the name. "That's almost as good as Richard Reason. Of course, if you want to do it properly, you could give him my middle name, too."

"What's that?" I asked.

"Idris," he confessed, and we all laughed.

And so we left Oxford and the past behind us and looked toward the promise of our future.

23. Forced Retreat

For four days the *Queen Elizabeth* boomed along through the great loneliness of the North Atlantic.

For Elisabeth, everything familiar and beloved lay far, far behind. With one tremendous wrench she had performed her act of faith, leaving family, friends, and nation, and put her future solely in my hands. For me, there was the fear of failing the trust she had placed in me, and the desperate uncertainty of how and where to begin building. There was no fixed point of reference from which to start, because I had no home—only a home town and a homeland. I would have to find a teaching job, but how and where? While still in Oxford,

I had written to the Dean at Harpur, which had been Triple Cities College, and to other colleges, but all had replied there were no vacancies. Where could I turn next?

On the fourth night, the heartbeats of the great ship died down to a murmur. On the morning of the fifth, she slipped along through the early fog into New York harbor. This was our new world, new for us both.

"Oh, darling, that must be New York! It's weird! It's fantastically beautiful!" We were standing on the top deck at six o'clock on the morning of July twenty-sixth, shivering slightly in the damp wind.

"What's so odd about it?" For me, New York had always been a roar and bustle with the smell of burnt gasoline and pizza and beer-soaked bars.

"It's like nothing I've ever seen before. You can just see the tops of what must be tall, slender buildings rising up out of the mist—a geometric pattern of spheres and pinnacles. And everything so sharp, so definite, as it comes out of the fog. It lies there between the sky and the fog, glistening in the sun, and keeps growing and changing as new peaks and spires appear—all shifting and spinning. All the vertical lines are soaring up and up and up toward the sun. It's like an imagination working.

"We must be getting closer now, and the mist is beginning to lift, too, and you can see more of each building. You can begin to see they do belong to a city—that they actually are based on earth. It's so different from home, where the cities run parallel with the land, horizontal lines only occasionally broken by a church tower or a steeple. It's so fantastic to see a glistening city hanging in midair and growing slowly down to the earth!"

This was my country; I was its child, but never before had I seen it until that morning. When the reality had materialized, it was, of course, a letdown from the view from the bay. We waited six hours in the broiling sun after the ship had docked before we could go ashore. Though I was a citizen and should have disembarked sooner, I was permitted to stay with Elisabeth, so I went off with the immigrants. I would have felt more like an immigrant, too, if it hadn't been for the familiar voices of Ken Whiting and his wife, Irene, shouting to me from the dock. They had driven down to meet us and take us back to Binghamton.

Finally we crawled out of the heat and the roaring confusion of New York, and Elisabeth saw for the first time the gleaming motels, drive-ins, and open-air stores with their large displays of bright, garish beachware in hard yellows, greens, and scarlets. The car radio blared the tight, nervous twitching of Rosemary Clooney calling out, "Come on to my house! Come on to my house!" When the hard afternoon sunlight had snapped off into night, we stopped at chrome restaurants with their droning fans and juke boxes from which Rosemary Clooney still cried her jerky invitation: "Come on to *my* house; come on to my *house;* come on to *my* house; come on to my *house*."

And then we were there. The car door was pulled open and Hunnie was climbing in to greet us.

Hunnie's husband Tom had just gone to Korea with the Army, so she had invited us to stay the rest of the summer with her and her two girls. There seemed to be no point in hunting for an apartment of our own because any day the mailman might bring me a job offer from one of the several colleges to which I had applied, and we would be leaving Binghamton. We didn't unpack.

The mailman came every day. He brought nothing but refusals.

August sweltered on and our hopes diminished as the pile of refusals grew. In spite of all Hunnie's kindness, the pleasure Elisabeth took in the two children, and the generous hospitality of friends, it was an unhappy time for us. For Elisabeth, Binghamton was not Cornwall, my family was not her family, and these people were not the people she had known and understood. On top of all this, we had no place to call our own, no specific tasks to occupy our time, no clear and definite future— nothing but dwindling hopes to hold on to.

Summer dragged along until the colleges had opened. There was no hope left. There were no high school jobs, either. I had investigated this possibility and learned that no visually handicapped person could teach in the New York State public schools. All applications to private schools met with rejections. There would be no teaching, then. Also, it now became clear that we would have to live in Binghamton for at least a year, so we rented a tiny apartment.

Though my memories of my early summer at I.B.M. were still unpleasantly green, I had to find some sort of job to tide us over until the next academic year. I went down again to their Endicott plant and made my application.

"I'm sorry. Things are very tight now. We can't take anyone on."

The story was the same everywhere. I tried all the twenty factories in the Triple Cities area—even though I knew by this time it would be useless. My blindness more than offset my degrees.

"It's really fantastic what you fellows can do," the personnel men would remark, "but . . ."

They thought of me just as most people think of "the blind"—I was utterly helpless or I was superhuman, and sometimes both at the same time. Either view tells equally against one when it comes to getting a job.

"I can't imagine how you have done what you have! It's really miraculous! But no, I won't give you a job turning a screw on our assembly line because I don't really think you could do it."

September passed, and October dragged itself along like a wounded snake.

"Something will turn up, darling; something's bound to turn up," Elisabeth encouraged.

"No. Nothing is going to turn up now."

"Oh, darling, why are people so stupid," she almost wept. "They're *so* stupid!"

"There's only one thing I can do now," I said to her. "I have to try to get a job at the Workshop for the Blind."

After all these years—after Hamilton, Yale, two years of teaching, and Oxford—to have to go back into a shelter! Since I had left the Institute I had been in open competition with sighted people, and now, when it really mattered, when I had a wife to look after and a whole new life to build, I was being forced back inch by inch, day by day, into the world from which I thought I had broken free.

Worst of all was being reminded of the shame—not the shame of defeat, but the deep and insidious shame of blindness. Being forced back into the workshop was to be reminded all over again of my inadequacy, all over again to clench my fists in impotent rage, to feel all over again the hot tears scald my cheeks. It was this shame I had yearned to escape from while I was at the Institute, and which the system of segregation so tragically reinforced. It was this of which my life during the last ten years had been so blessedly free—exorcised by friendship and love.

To go into the workshop was to go back into the system, with all it implied. But I had no choice. I went to my old friend, Mrs. Mary K. De Witt.

"Sure, I'll give you a job. That's what the shop is for. I'm sorry you need us, but I'm glad we can help. Things have changed since you wove pocketbooks for us. We have a new building down on Water Street. It's a regular factory. Our bread and butter is the subcontract work we get from I.B.M., so I expect you'll be doing exactly the same sort of job as an I.B.M. worker, but, of course, you won't be getting their pay. Do you want to start tomorrow?" And it was settled.

We worked from seven in the morning until four in the afternoon, with an hour off for lunch. The work could have been worse, I might have been kept on one job, such as putting in tabs on the time-card racks. Fortunately, nobody suffered that particular kind of torture at the workshop, because our subcontracted work kept changing. The jobs might take three weeks or one week or perhaps only two days, and most of them were different. When the I.B.M. truck rolled up to unload, activities slowed down and you could fairly hear people listening. If the truck brought only a small job, there would be idle hands, and idle hands meant shorter hours, and shorter hours meant even leaner pay checks.

Fortunately, the truck kept us pretty busy. Frequently the jobs were assembling parts. For example, we were given plastic panels, some four inches wide and seven inches long. They had about fourteen rows of holes, with thirty holes to a row. We had to put bolts in only certain holes. We would slip all the bolts into the proper holes, and then the trick was to flip the panel over without letting the bolts fall out, so we could put on washers and nuts. Sometimes we had to put on one washer and sometimes two; sometimes one nut and sometimes two. We would start the nuts on all the bolts and then zip them down tight with our high-speed wrenches, operated by compressed air. The finished panels were complicated patterns of nuts and bolts—contact panels for calculators.

This went on day after day, week after week, month after month, for eight hours a day.

My experience of years before at I.B.M. had taught me the danger of this kind of work: its tendency to paralyze the mind. I was desperately afraid of losing my mental energy, so Elisabeth and I worked a regular reading program into our day.

We got up at five-thirty and, while I showered and shaved, Elisabeth had her breakfast so she could read to me while I ate mine. We read until six-forty-three, when I left to catch my bus at the corner. When I came home at four-thirty, Elisabeth usually had dinner ready so we had a good long evening in which to read again. Thus, while my outer ear buzzed with the whine and burr of air wrenches, my inner ear rejoiced in the turn of a sentence from Jane Austen or Charlotte Brontë. We read all the Brontë novels that winter and dipped back into the eighteenth century, too.

The winter of 1951 and the spring and summer of 1952 was a time of anger and frustration for both of us, but it had its other side. The very circumstances that oppressed our hearts also brought them closer together. In those long evenings when I wrote letters of application, and in those dolorous sessions of reading refusals, we learned how long and how desperately we would have to struggle. Until now I had fought to escape shame for my own sake; now I fought so that Elisabeth would not have to share it.

And just before that Christmas of 1951 the doctor told us our child would arrive about the first of the following August. Now it wasn't only ourselves; it was our family. There was no question about it. I simply had to get a teaching job.

Since we were going to have a baby, and since I thought it would be embarrassing to have to change diapers on the train while we were traveling to that job, there seemed only one answer.

"You know what I think? I think we need a car."

"What for?" Elisabeth exclaimed. "I can't drive, and anyway we can't afford it."

Her question was an easy one to answer: It would be fun. That Elisabeth couldn't drive presented some obstacles, I had to admit; but the last point was a devastating one.

Our income amounted to thirty-five dollars a week, fifteen of which went for rent. Four or five dollars more went for stationery, envelopes, stamps, typewriter ribbons, and so on. Five or six more disappeared into the coffers of various insurance companies. After we subtracted from the remaining ten dollars what was essential for such incidentals as food and clothing, we squandered the rest on high living. We had what Dickens would have called "a snug little establishment," and it would have taken a Dickens, too, to describe the pleasure we took in, and the ceremonious courtesy with which we greeted, a bit of meat on our table.

Owning a car wasn't really a very practical proposition and I had a very practical wife. However, arguments could be marshaled.

"When we get the job," I began confidently, "we must have a car to take us there. We'll save the cost of the car on that trip alone. Now is the time to learn how to drive, before the baby comes, and the only way to learn is to have our own car. Besides, it would be such fun!" I thought these very powerful arguments.

It was a '39 Ford station wagon.

When we put in a new master cylinder, new brake lines and linings, and a few other small things, it would stop as well as start. As the result of much practice, the combined instruction of our friends, and most especially the result of my careful explanations of the art of driving, Elisabeth failed her test. She was so miserable that she called me at the shop in the middle of the morning to weep the news. I consoled her by promising to explain all the fine points I had omitted. By the time I reached home, her fighting spirit was up. She wouldn't listen to anything I said, so the following week she passed the test and received her license.

As Elisabeth had predicted, we couldn't afford the car; but as I had predicted, it was great fun. We took the seats out of the back, put in an old mattress, our fishing equipment, a gasoline lantern, and a Coleman stove. Every Friday afternoon at four we left Binghamton to spend the week end fishing, reading, sun-bathing, and swimming. And for two full days there was no tiny dark apartment in the early morning, and no radio hooting: "Shrimpboats are a-comin', there'll be dancin' tonight," no shop with the whir and buzz of compressors and air wrenches.

"Set a meditative man upon his legs and he will lead you to water," says Melville. Put two young people in love into an old station wagon fitted out for camping, and they won't lead anybody to water, but they'll find it for themselves.

And each time it was different—the low, swift Delaware rushing along between steep, rocky, and wooded banks; the sleepy Susquehanna moving placidly through hayfields and corn; or the branches of the Chenango with riffs and rapids like the Delaware's and long quiet stretches of still, deep water. We drove down old overgrown cart tracks to the river's edge and made our camp on the rocks. We woke in the showers of predawn dew, fished and cooked breakfast with the morning redwings for music, and once, in the Adirondacks, the sweet call of the white-throated sparrow.

This was old familiar country to me, but it was all new and strange for Elisabeth, and so it also became new for me, just as New York City had become a different place because of her.

One week end in the middle of July we left the rivers to explore the back country and the little trout streams. We camped beside an old deserted farmhouse covered with wisteria. Through the knee-high grass in the front yard we walked around to the back, where there were still faint outlines of a flower garden in the wilderness of weeds. The gaunt, rusty skeleton of an old pump leaned precariously over the sagging well cover. What ghosts from the past whispered about us! They had loved this old house, with its fragrant garden sloping down to the creek. Time and weeds and weather had softened and mellowed the place, and now there was not so much evidence of life as there was room for the imagination.

"Oh, look, there's a horseshoe," Elisabeth cried with sudden pleasure, and she picked it up. "We must keep it. This is a lovely place, and I want to remember it. Anyway, horseshoes bring good luck."

There are places for superstition, and this was one of them.

The following Sunday afternoon about four o'clock, just in time for tea but four days before we could claim maternity benefits from our Blue Cross policy, Richard Russell presented himself to two very proud and very happy new parents—not Richard Idris, but Richard Geoffrey.

"He's so beautiful! So beautiful!" Elisabeth sighed drowsily as she was wheeled out and onto the hospital elevator. "You see, it's that horseshoe," and we were both overcome by the blessedness of it, the miracle of birth, the marvelous newbornness of our own son.

My week's vacation from the workshop coincided perfectly with Elisabeth's coming home from the hospital. During that week I was the doting father and husband. I had dishpan hands, housemaid's knee, and a good start on a chronic backache. On top of this, I couldn't sleep.

Either Elisabeth or I would wake up two or three times every night, steal quietly out into the living room to lean over Richie's bassinet, and listen to make sure he was still breathing. It all seemed so wonderful to have a real, live child of our own. We were such green parents we didn't then realize he wasn't ours at all, except when he bumped his head or scraped his knee. The rest of the time he belonged to himself, and soon he wouldn't even come to us about the bumps.

I went back to the shop wearing what I hoped looked like a benign paternal air. On the Thursday of that first week I came home to find that Elisabeth had put Richie in his carriage and was wheeling him out into the pocket-handkerchief back yard.

"Do you think he'll be all right out there?" I asked. "By himself, you know?"

"Of course he will," Elisabeth replied. "What could possibly happen to him?"

"Nothing, I suppose. Nothing, of course. Still, didn't you say you saw a squirrel out there last week?"

"Yes. That's right, I did. Do you think squirrels—"

"No, of course not. That is, I don't think so. Squirrels aren't generally . . . at least I never heard . . . Hey! He sneezed! Did you hear that? Maybe he's catching cold. Don't you think we'd better . . . ?"

"Well, perhaps we had."

So we wheeled him back, and I carefully lifted the carriage up the steps and through the door. Just then the phone rang. I picked it up. "Hello."

"Hello. I have a call from Chicago for a Robert Russell."

"Yes. This is Robert Russell." Elisabeth froze in the doorway.

"What is it, darling?"

"Chicago. They must have the wrong Robert Russell, though." We waited breathlessly.

After an eternity the operator said, "Hello. I have your party for you, sir. Go ahead, please."

"Hello, Robert Russell?"

"Yes, speaking."

"This is President A. J. Brumbaugh. A letter of application sent to the University of Chicago has been referred to me by Dean Ward. I am the President of Shimer College in northwestern Illinois. We are closely affiliated with the University of Chicago, and we are looking for an English instructor for this coming autumn. Are you still available?"

Available! I had never been so available in all my life! Though my head was swimming, I kept saying,

"Yes . . . yes . . . yes, yes," until President Brumbaugh hung up.

"Quick, quick! Tell me!" Elisabeth cried.

"Well, it's nothing, really. I mean I haven't got the job, of course. No cause for celebration. He's coming East to Yale, and I am to see him there for an interview next Tuesday. There are other candidates, you know . . . he knows I'm blind, though . . . let's call Hunnie . . . I don't suppose for one moment there's a chance . . . too early for a party or anything . . . get the Whitings . . . it's a permanent job, too . . . what's Bill Johnson's number . . . where's the opener?"

I suppose I did work the next day. I also had a haircut and bought a suit.

Then to New Haven, the interview, and home again on air.

"I haven't got the job, darling—not for certain. He has other people to see . . . but he seemed pretty final. He said he'd call me when he got back to wherever it is and after he had talked with his trustees and advisers. That won't be until next Monday. I don't suppose I have a chance, but he did seem very interested. He says there's an apartment waiting for us. My blindness didn't seem to bother him much. Naturally, he asked all sorts of questions, but he was very fair. Let's go down to the cellar and get out the trunks."

Monday came, the call came, and then the contract.

24. Round Trip

I don't suppose journeys into the Midwest necessarily have to be made in Jabberwockies and the descendants of Jabberwockies. Other people go in things that look more like cars and act more like cars. The station wagon took it well, though, or at least it took 850 of the nine hundred miles well. It went lame on the last fifty, but it went.

All day long we drove into the fierce sunshine. Down in one of the crevices of luggage behind the front seat our five-week-old Richie lay in his bassinet, rocked to sleep by the swaying of the station wagon. We stopped in little shady roadside parks to feed and change him and to study our maps.

It seemed fantastic that we could climb into our sta-

tion wagon and, with nothing but a few lines and numbers on odd bits of paper, cover almost a thousand miles
of country entirely strange to both of us and actually
find at the end a little town we had never heard of until
three weeks before.

In the evenings we stopped at the cheapest motel we
could find, had dinner, bathed Richie, and tried to sleep.
All night long the huge trucks swept past outside like
sudden avalanches along the road. Everyone seemed to
be on the move—a constant and perpetual transition.
We were on the move, too, a part of what the shifting
skyline of New York symbolized. It was exciting and a
little frightening.

On the evening of the fourth day, a sign declared that
we were approaching Mount Carroll. On top of a hill
overlooking the village we stopped, got out, and
stretched ourselves, drinking in the cool country air. We
washed as well as we could with what was left of the jug
of drinking water.

"We have to look presentable, you know," Elisabeth
said, "even if we aren't. They are getting a bargain in
us, nevertheless. What do you suppose it will be like?"

"I have nothing but composition—four sections of it
—so there'll be millions of essays, but there won't be any
more workshop, and there won't be any more of those
damned 'shrimpboats a-comin'' at five-thirty in the
morning. It will be hard work for you, though, reading
all those essays to me. We'll have our hands full, but it's
our start. We will be making our living by reading and
talking about what we have read, and what could be
more wonderful than that?"

Just then the wind changed and we got our first evidence that pig farming was very popular thereabouts.

"Come on, then!—though the start of a new life would be more romantic if we didn't squeak and rattle quite so much and if the sweet country air were a little sweeter."

For the next few days we received courtesy calls from the rest of the faculty and their wives. They came with offerings from their gardens: baskets of tomatoes, corn, beets, and beans. We entertained them with cups of hot tea amid a jumble of packing cases.

Our apartment seemed immense—four huge rooms with great, long windows. Outside stood a catalpa tree, whose large waxy flowers and unusual fragrance became a familiar June smell. On our left lay the neat, pleasant college campus—brick buildings, paved walks crisscrossing wide lawns, tall, leafy shade trees. To our right stretched the little country town, the county seat of a farming community. It had its brick courthouse, small shops, A & P, and large old Victorian frame houses set among lawns and trees on the outskirts. Farther out rose the corncribs, silver silos, and red barns of Midwestern farms, and ten miles farther west rolled the wide Mississippi.

During that first year of our escape, the freedom was inexpressibly sweet. Elisabeth and I worked long, long hours together. We learned to share each other's tasks. Together we did the housework so Elisabeth would have time to read.

Shimer was then closely affiliated with the University

of Chicago, whose undergraduate division was given over to the Hutchins Plan of General Education. At Shimer we taught exactly the same courses as at the university and our students took the same examinations. The difference was that, at the end of their program at Shimer, our students received degrees from Shimer instead of from the University of Chicago. Since they were doing the same work and being graded by the same standards, even the not very bright students could see the advantages of transferring to Chicago for their degree. As a result, our student body was not large.

But even those few students seemed a lot to me. I had practically all of them for English composition. A huge pile of essays seemed always to be sitting on the corner of my desk, and these, plus the demands of our growing Richie, plus the fact that my salary was minute, meant we had neither the time nor the money for even a reasonable amount of dissipation. We made it to one movie that first year; as for alcohol, we were driven to brewing our own.

My sister Mary had given us her recipe for making beer. She had six children then, so she was very adept at such little economies.

"It only costs about eight cents a quart to make," she explained, "and one quart of it will do the work of three quarts of the commercial product."

She was right on both counts.

Our brew brought us a good deal of acclaim. The most appreciative of our regular guests was Merlin Bowen, the head of the Humanities Department. He was on loan to Shimer from the University of Chicago faculty, and through him I came to know many of his Chicago colleagues.

In my second year I was relieved of some of the burden of composition in order to take on work in the humanities with Merlin. I wasn't being paid much at Shimer, but for all I learned through working with Merlin, I felt as though I should have been paying the college for making him available. We held our department meetings while walking home for lunch together or over a couple of bottles of home brew in the evening or, after payday, down at Poffy's Tavern, the local Democratic headquarters. The only thing we needed for a department meeting was a copy of the book we were teaching, and Merlin always seemed to have that.

Though the winters were raw and bleak and the summers stifling, spring and fall were marvelous. We would bundle up Richie, strap him into his stroller, and off we would go for long walks in the country. We didn't have to plod through the usual jungle of gas stations, factories, warehouses, used-car lots, and motels. In five minutes we could be leaning on a pasture fence trying to entice the calves over with bunches of grass so Richie could get a good look.

In the autumn we went nutting. We had found a few black-walnut trees.

"Are they good?" Elisabeth asked.

"They're great!" I cried. "We must go home and get some baskets or boxes or something. We'll lay in a real supply for the spring."

"The spring!" Elisabeth exclaimed.

"Oh, yes. You have to let them dry out all winter."

We struggled back and forth across the fields with heavy baskets. The nuts dried out all winter on the radiator in the downstairs hallway. The following July I took three nuts out onto the sidewalk, where, after fifteen minutes, I managed to crack them. Two were empty and the third was wormy. The rest dried out on the radiator for two more years before we threw them away.

Not all our expeditions into the country were fruitless, however. We spent many happy afternoons with Merlin, his wife Ruth, and their two boys, picnicking together in the Palisades State Park along the Mississippi. Under the influence of sunshine, fresh air, and charcoaled hamburgers, Merlin could sometimes be persuaded to talk about Herman Melville, about whom he was writing his doctoral thesis.

Though I scarcely knew enough about Melville to ask intelligent questions, I had written a thesis myself, so I had some idea of how much sympathy Merlin deserved. To read Melville was a joy, and sometimes even Melville's critics were exciting; but the actual writing! There lay the chore. To talk is pleasant and easy, even stimulating; but to sit down, put a piece of paper into a typewriter, and then to make sense—that was a different thing.

"Each clear sentence is that much ground stripped clean of the undergrowth of one's own confusion. Sometimes it's thrilling to feel you have written even a single paragraph that makes sense," I declared sanctimoniously.

One afternoon Elisabeth heard me holding forth. That

evening after dinner while I was drying the dishes, she said, "I heard you telling Merlin about the satisfactions of writing. Why don't you write a book?"

"Me! Write a book! What about?"

"Oh, if you can't think of anything better, write about yourself." She paused. "That's it: Write an autobiography."

I thought about it for a moment. I had always been in transit before. Now that we had arrived, in a sense, perhaps it was time to survey the country I had traveled. "That's not such a bad idea," I answered. "Perhaps it is time. But we must have a place, a quiet, lovely place. There must be a lake or a river, and I must go out alone to fish. The place must be ours, too. It must belong to us."

I had always responded to the sounds of wind and water. The pleasantest memories of my growing had been bound up with a boat rocking at anchor and the sudden nervous, electric charge of life along the line I had tossed into the unknown. Indeed, fishing is for me a sort of symbol of living.

To our solitary vessels, adrift in open time, we feel without any warning the sudden charge of energy telling us we are not alone in the universe—it may be a line of poetry that penetrates the heart, or a gesture, or the tone of a voice revealing in another the secret we had imagined to be all our own. The mystery of self is repeated over and over again and lies hidden beneath the surface of the familiar. But it usually takes a crisis to make us look beneath that surface.

In my case, it was the grief I felt at my father's death

that burned through the layers of the familiar and opened my eyes to the person he had really been. Until then it had not occurred to me to ask what manner of man he was; so, in a sense, it was not until his death that I began to know him.

> "Full fathom five thy father lies;
>   Of his bones are coral made:
> Those are pearls that were his eyes:
>   Nothing of him that doth fade,
> But doth suffer a sea-change
> Into something rich and strange."

It was my father's death that led me to discover him as a person and then to discover literature, which contains what is rich and strange in human nature—all that lies full fathom five below the prosaic surface on which we pass our ordinary, everyday lives. Through literature I found humanity, and began at last to find my self.

It lay deeply buried beneath the familiar and beneath the layers of secrecy with which I had instinctively hidden it not only from the gaze of others, but even from my own. The writing of such a book would mean a retracing of my steps, recapturing at each period of my life the different persons I had been. Now that I thought the self had ceased its posings and disguises and was more or less committed to a stable identity, I had to go back, to ferret out, to capture, to analyze, and to understand what I had been so I could understand my self, so I could achieve quiet possession of the self—so I could know what I really was.

When I had begun to think through my past during

that third year at Mount Carroll, I happened to learn through mutual friends that Faith, with her husband and children, was then living up in the lake country of Wisconsin some three hundred miles north of us. I wrote asking her if we could come and stay with them while we looked for our quiet place to read and fish and write.

"Please come," she answered, and we did.

Faith and I met once more, and not on the terms on which we had parted years before or with melancholy memories of our happy times together. She was secure and happy in her marriage, and I could not imagine life without Elisabeth. No scent of faded rose petals hung in the air between us. There were no traces of regret for either of us.

It was indeed time to write the book.

We had come prepared to hunt seriously for a cottage. With great care we had studied the articles in *Consumer's Report* on how houses should be examined and rated. We had carefully abstracted all the important points from the articles, set them up in columns, and I had typed them on a master sheet from which we ran off thirty or forty copies—most of which we subsequently lost. Equipped with these sheets, a pencil, flashlight, tape measure, and penknife, we set about annoying the real-estate men up there in the lake country. We were insufferable!

"Now, this is a particularly nice place," the salesman remarked as we drew up by a tar-paper shack.

"Virgin timber, this. Come here, Mr. Russell. I want you to feel this tree. I bet it's eighty feet tall."

"It's the house . . ."

"This is Bass Lake, right here, and I guess you know how that got its name," he chuckled suggestively. "Yes, sir, I was showing another party around the other day, and I tossed out a line and got a six-pounder. Some fishing here!"

"We want to see the house," I insisted.

"Well, now, it's not a palace, you know," and he laughed good-naturedly as he reluctantly opened the door. "There's your stove, dishes, a couple of beds— usual cabin furniture. You don't really need much in that way in a cottage."

"Got the tape measure, Elisabeth? Let's just measure the distance between these studs."

"Oh, that! They're a little wide, but it's just cottage-built, you know."

"They're thirty inches apart," Elisabeth declared firmly. "That's a minus four on the chart."

"They ought to be on sixteen-inch centers," I remarked severely to nobody in particular.

"Well, it's not all that important," the salesman said, trying to cajole me.

"Let's have a look at the foundation," I suggested. "The floor seems to sag pretty badly here."

"There really isn't any foundation. It's just up on cedar posts," the salesman explained, trying to keep the annoyance out of his voice. We went outside. I took my knife and tested the posts. The blade sank in up to the hilt.

"Mmm!" I said darkly.

"It's soft wood. Cedar *is* soft wood!" he defended.

"Mmm!" I said again, even more darkly.

"This floor joist," Elisabeth observed, sticking her head out from beneath the house, "is only a two-by-six, and it's pretty soft, too."

"Oh, that's nothing—nothing at all. It's no job just to jack her up and slip another joist in there—takes about fifteen minutes. A fellow who knew what he was doing . . ."

"And you said they want forty-five hundred for this?" I asked with obvious incredulity.

"Well," and he began to hedge good-humoredly, "now that's the asking price. You know how it is—a fellow can *ask* anything he wants. I don't blame him, either; but I think I could make him listen to reason. I'll give the owner a call this afternoon, if you say so, and I think we could probably swing it for about four thousand. There is a little work to be done on the place."

"Sorry. That's no good."

"Well, maybe I could get him down to thirty-five for you."

"No. We don't really want it."

"All right. You're the boss. Whatever you say. Virgin timber, though."

We climbed back into his car and went on to see more "virgin timber" and still more "virgin timber," but *Consumer's Report* had forewarned us about things like "virgin timber." We were so cautious that we went away without buying anything at all. Despondently we left for Mount Carroll, having measured the distance between the studs of half the cabins in the lake country and poked our knife into countless rotten cedar posts.

"Anyway, darling, don't be disappointed. We're not

going to stay in Mount Carroll much longer. We might be going to Arizona, for all we know, and then what good would a cabin up here be?"

Elisabeth was right. We had found security in Mount Carroll, and so we had to leave. As I had left Hamilton for Yale, Yale for teaching, teaching for Oxford, the pattern was being repeated.

Even before going up to the lakes, we had started to send out letters of application. The college in Mount Carroll was too small to have any future for me, I thought. It had given me the start I needed, but I had to be moving on, and I had long since learned that, if I wanted to get a job, I had to go looking for it.

The first step was to send out letters as before, describing my background and qualifications and explaining how I managed what they might think were problems. The second was to keep the polite refusals until the middle of the following November. The third was to write to the people who had politely refused, telling them I was going to be at the Modern Language Association's convention in New York City after Christmas and that, from their letters, they seemed to be such nice people, I would consider it a pleasure if they would join me for dinner or lunch at some time during the three-day convention. The fourth step was supposed to be their replying that, since *I* seemed such a nice chap from my letters, they would love to have lunch with me on Tuesday; and then the fifth step was supposed to be my inducing them to produce a contract over dessert.

We began this operation early in the spring and continued it throughout the rest of the year. Not that I wrote invitations to dinner for the rest of the year, but we prepared ourselves for the major part of the campaign—the trip to New York—by saving our money. We resorted to all sorts of economies, the main secret of which consisted in not buying anything.

We got a small plot of ground from one of the neighbors and had a vegetable garden. The neighbor was very reluctant to let us have this plot because he was certain we would let it go to ruin and, since his garden was right next to it, our weeds would march over and strangle his cucumbers.

He was wrong, though, which made him exceedingly annoyed. Ours was a picture-book garden. The rows were crooked, but there wasn't a weed to be seen anywhere—anywhere, that is, except in his plot. We had a bumper crop of everything. Our tomatoes flowered before his, our corn tasseled and ripened before his, and our string beans didn't seem to know when to stop. We even had to rent two lockers at the frozen-food plant. Finally, in a fit of understandable exasperation, our landlord tore out everything that remained in our plot and flung it over the fence to his sheep. But we didn't mind; we had all we could use.

Elisabeth sewed and patched, patched and sewed, and when we entertained, which was seldom, we did so with home-brew or tea, according to the respectability of our guests.

In the middle of November I sent the lunch and dinner invitations to a select group of twenty-five polite department heads—but not without some misgivings. At the most, the three-day conference could offer nine meals, and there were twenty-five prospective partners.

"If everybody accepts," Elisabeth suggested, "you'll have to serve a buffet luncheon in your room."

It turned out not to be necessary, of course, although on one day I did find myself with three separate luncheon engagements for twelve-fifteen. The replies trickled in. Nobody had been fooled by the invitation; it was pretty thin.

"Thank you for your invitation, but I'm sorry, we don't expect to have any vacancies next year. Good luck."

"Actually we do have an instructorship going for next year, but there's no need for you to bribe me with lunch or dinner or even cocktails. Here is my room number. Get in touch with me there, and we can have a quiet chat."

"We do expect to hire someone next year, and I would be glad to have lunch with you on Wednesday, say, at twelve-fifteen. Let's meet at the Information Booth on the first floor."

One of my luncheon dates was with Professor M. Ray Adams, head of the English Department at Franklin and Marshall College in Lancaster, Pennsylvania. We had a pleasant chat. Mr. Adams explained that they were looking for someone with training in the nineteenth century and also for someone who could do some teaching in their humanities sequence. As we talked on, it became increasingly clear to me it was a job I would like, and that my training and experience qualified me for serious consideration.

"You understand I am not empowered to make you a definite offer," Mr. Adams said. "We have a joint faculty and administrative committee that does all the hiring at the level of assistant professor and above, so you will have to be interviewed by them. Could you come to Lancaster for an interview perhaps early in March?"

Returning from the convention, I stepped off the train in Mount Carroll. Elisabeth rushed up with, "Well?"

"We must get out the trunks again!" I said jubilantly.

We packed most of our things even before the interview, and this time most of the burden lay upon my shoulders. Our second son, Mark Robert, was only a few weeks from making his entrance into the world, and an exciting and excited household it was when he came. When he was only two weeks old I made the long journey to Lancaster for my interview. All went well and I returned to Mount Carroll with a definite offer.

"Tell me!" Elisabeth cried. "How did it go?"

"We've got to pack," I answered happily.

"We already have," she reminded me.

We left Mount Carroll as soon as I had marked the last exam. By this time we were old hands at traveling. We put complete faith in our maps, but this time it was Mark whom we hauled out of a crevice in the luggage.

The college had rented us a house near the campus; so, at four o'clock one June morning, we found ourselves driving around Lancaster chasing milkmen to get directions from them. At last we arrived and walked into a rose-filled garden just as the first robin started his morning song.

25. Unquiet Possession

"We mustn't forget that quiet place," I said to Elisabeth. "We're back pretty close to my part of the country, and I think I know where we ought to look."

"Where?"

"The St. Lawrence River. I went there once a long time ago. I was thirteen. It was where I first fell in love, and I'd like to take you back there."

Before college opened in the fall, we drove up to the St. Lawrence. It was still the great sleepy giant of seventeen years before, and the big, soft, fresh wind still boomed down out of Canada. Elisabeth loved it as I had loved it—the great sweeps of open water that challenge as they fulfill, and challenge again. And, on an island about a mile and a half off the Canadian shore, she said, "This is our place; yes, this is beautiful; this is where we belong."

We didn't have our test sheets any more. We didn't have our tape measure, our flashlight, or our penknife; we didn't even ask if the roof leaked. You don't need to know that when you find the place.

We went back to the mainland in the water taxi, talked over how we could scrape the money together, and then went back to Hay Island, our island.

"We've decided to take the cottage," I said to the owner.

It wasn't quite as simple as all that. There had been others to see the place, there had been half promises, they were partially committed . . . and on and on. They would let us know. We learned the next day that the place wasn't for sale. Heartbroken, we made the long trip back to our new home in Lancaster.

As the year went along we forgot our disappointment, or at least the worst of it, because the new job was all I hoped it would be and more. Though I had very much enjoyed the teaching at Shimer, nevertheless the courses in General Education prevented the instructor from doing any teaching in his own special field. At Franklin and Marshall I taught an advanced course in English prose of the Victorian era. It seemed like coming home again to get back to Cardinal Newman, Ruskin, Pater, and the others.

In April I sent a note to the real-estate man in Canada who had shown us our place, asking him to keep us in mind. He answered immediately, saying there was another larger, cheaper, and better cottage for sale on the same island. In spite of all the wise cautions of *Consumer's Report,* and directly contrary to all the dictates of ordinary common sense, we bought it without even seeing it.

And it has become our place, our quiet place.

We are on Hay Island, which, at least four or five families agree, is the loveliest of the Thousand Islands. Ours is a two-and-a-half-story cottage with a large front porch facing west. In front and to our left lie the Wide Waters, a seven-mile open stretch running all the way to the American shore. At our end of the Wide Waters lies the famous Forty Acre Shoal, the fabled home of the mighty muskelunge. The prevailing winds are southwesterly, so they sweep across the Wide Waters and the Forty Acres to send great, rolling whitecaps crashing up the granite cliffs of the little islands lying directly in front of us. When the river becomes wild, it is like the sea along the coast of Cornwall, and then, at other times, it is mirror-smooth like my Chenango. In my early teens, all the tumult and uncertainty lay in me and not in the waters I sailed upon. Now it is different.

So that I can go out by myself whenever I please, I have run a wire down to the end of the dock, where I have mounted a large electric bell. Before I go down to the dock, I plug the line into an outlet in the house. A timing device permits the bell to ring only once every thirty seconds. If I row too far upwind to be able to hear the bell, I can still fish without anxiety because I can always drift downwind, and then I am again in touch with my base.

And a man needs a base to quest from, and he needs the sense that, however far he has strayed, return is still possible. Confidence that he has such a base is all that gives him the courage to reach past the edges of the familiar. It may be what he knows, what he believes, the table round, or Heaven itself. The river lies before me, a constant invitation, a constant challenge, and my bell is the thread of sound along which I return.

To a quiet base.

Quiet? Not altogether, even though, on looking at the deed to the cottage, we found that the Crown guarantees us in no uncertain terms: "quiet possession of the said lands."

There are bats. They sleep all day, it's true, but when we are trying to sleep, they are holding pep rallies, conventions, and football games up in the attic. Sometimes it sounds as if they are having public meetings to discuss how they can get rid of the humans who have moved in down below.

And wasps. Everyone can expect to meet a wasp or two in the course of a full and rich life, and, while a sting hurts for a while, it passes off—only it doesn't pass off in Elisabeth's case. She is violently allergic to stings, and since one bad scare, she has had to carry a hypodermic of adrenalin around in her pocket in case she is stung.

There was the boat, too, and the cursed motor.

Our first year we had a twelve-foot car-top boat weighing only sixty-five pounds. It was just the thing for two careful boys on a duckpond, but not the sort of boat for the St. Lawrence. With Elisabeth and me, the two children, groceries, a big cake of ice, and a secondhand motor that wouldn't work, there was about an inch of freeboard between the gunwale and the waterline. And then, of course, there's the dog, which doesn't like riding in a boat, but which won't stay home by himself and won't sit still. And the tour boats, great big things, go roaring by, throwing up tremendous waves. . . .

And there's the camp—a girls' camp. Somebody over on the point of Hay Island sold his estate to a worthy organization that set up a camp for young girls—seventy-five of them, from eight through fifteen. At night they all go creeping around through the brush, hunting for something or other and laughing and giggling and hooting and hollering. Early every morning they all get together and sing, "Holy, Holy, Holy!"

We have had hurricanes, too.

I don't even know whom I can sue as having trespassed on my rights to "quiet possession of the said lands." I wouldn't stand a chance if I took that girls' camp to court—their motives are all so upstanding and commendable. The bats and the wasps and the big black ants that are eating out the joists from under the back porch wouldn't even appear.

And Mark and Richie go running through the living room and dining room screaming with delight because they've got old cigar boxes on their feet and they're water-skiing; and the dog is yelping to be let in; and Porgy, the parakeet, is chattering away at the top of his voice trying to drown out everybody else; and now there are two more children, James and Miranda.

It makes me wonder if there is any such thing as "quiet possession of the said"—or of any other—"lands."

The truth of the matter is there is no such thing as "quiet possession" of anything—not anything alive—and it's only an idle boast of some lawyer or maybe the Queen to pretend they can guarantee it.

On the other hand, who would really want "quiet possession"? Perhaps quiet possession is not such a good thing after all, because that would mean that the thing you possessed would have to be dead.

I have said earlier that one of the reasons I wrote this book was because I wanted to secure some quiet possession of my self, because originally I had thought it was possible. Especially, I thought I could do this because I had arrived at a fixed point of reference from which to view the muddle of the past. But now I know, looking back through the events and experiences I have set down, that I can see many different selves I have not described at all—selves that pop out at me from behind conclusions I thought were watertight.

The self will not be quietly possessed. Its living substance slips and slides through nets of words. Only an outline can be traced here and there, a silhouette against the background of experience. But if this is true, what have I gained from my quest?

This, I think.

In my life I see the age-old pattern of growth, the pattern of the crab. What I had imagined to be only a metaphor now seems to me to be a truth. My blindness has made me more acutely conscious of the attractions of my old shells, and so the fear of death has driven me through and from them perhaps more swiftly than it does most men. My quest began as the quest of Narcissus

—the search for the gaudy vessel of my ego. Gradually it became the quest for the Grail, the chalice containing the secret of Man.

And to seek to possess this is to try to catch the last of all the angels.